COVENANT • BIBLE • STUDIES

Side by Side
Interpreting Dual Stories in the Bible

Frank Ramirez

faithQuest® ♦ Brethren Press®

Side by Side: Interpreting Dual Stories in the Bible
Covenant Bible Studies Series

Copyright © 2005 by *faithQuest*®. Published by Brethren Press®, 1451 Dundee Avenue, Elgin, IL 60120.

Brethren Press and *faithQuest* are trademarks of the Church of the Brethren General Board.

Unless otherwise noted, scripture quotations are from the New Revised Standard Version of the Bible, copyrighted 1989 by the National Council of Churches of Christ in the USA, Division of Education and Ministry.

Cover photo: D. Jeanene Tiner

09 08 07 06 05   5 4 3 2 1

Library of Congress Control Number: 2005927168
ISBN-13: 978-0-87178-066-9
ISBN-10: 0-87178-066-6

Manufactured in the United States of America

Contents

Foreword

The Covenant Bible Study Series provides relational Bible studies for people who want to study the Bible in small groups rather than alone.

Relational Bible study is marked by certain characteristics that differ from other types of Bible study. We are reminded that relational Bible study is anchored in covenantal history. God covenanted with people in Old Testament history, established a new covenant in Jesus Christ, and covenants with the church today. Thus, this Bible study is intended for small groups of people who can meet face-to-face on a regular basis and share frankly and covenant with one another in an intimate group.

Relational Bible study takes seriously a corporate faith. As each person contributes to study, prayer, and work, the group becomes the real body of Christ. Each one's contribution is needed and important. "For just as the body in one and has many members, and all the members of the body, though many, are one body, so it is with Christ. . . . Now you are the body of Christ and individually members of it" (1 Cor. 12:12, 17).

Relational Bible study helps both individuals and the group to claim the promise of the Spirit and the working of the Spirit. As one person testified, "In our commitment to one another and in our sharing, something happened. . . .we were woven together in love by the Master Weaver. It is something that can happen only when two or three or seven are gathered in God's name, and we know the promise of God's presence in our lives.

In the small group environment, the members aid one another in seeking to become

- biblically informed so they better understand the revelation of God;

• globally aware so they know themselves to be better connected with all of God's world;
• relationally sensitive to God, self, and others.

For people who choose to use this study in a small group, the following intentions will help create an atmosphere in which support will grow and faith will deepen.

1. As a small group of learners, we gather around God's word to discern its meaning for today.
2. The words, stories, and admonitions we find in scripture come alive for today, challenging and renewing us.
3. All people are learners and all are leaders.
4. Each person will contribute to the study, sharing the meaning found in the scripture and helping to bring meaning to others.
5. We recognize each other's vulnerability as we share out of our own experience, and in sharing we learn to trust others and to be trustworthy.

The questions in the Suggestions for Sharing and Prayer section are intended for use in the hour preceding the Bible study to foster intimacy in the covenant group and to relate personal sharing to the Bible study topic, preparing one another to go out again in all directions to be in the world.

Welcome to this study. As you search the scriptures, may you also search yourself. May God's voice and guidance and the love and encouragement of brothers and sisters in Christ challenge you to live more fully the abundant life God promises.

Preface

A scene in Beverly Cleary's book *Ramona the Pest* hit home as I began to write this book.

Ramona's first day of kindergarten was off to a slow start when the teacher, Miss Binney, decided to read *Mike Mulligan and His Steam Shovel* to the class. It's the story of an old-fashioned steam shovel that's about to be junked. But thanks to Mike Mulligan, who works from dawn to dusk, the pair is able to excavate a basement for the town hall in the face of a looming deadline.

After the story is over, Ramona asks an obvious question—how did Mike Mulligan go to the bathroom? As it turns out, the rest of the class was wondering the same thing.

The embarrassed teacher finally admits that she does not know. "The book doesn't tell us," she responds.

This doesn't stop the children from speculating. One child suggests that Mike Mulligan probably just stopped working, climbed out of the hole, and visited a nearby gas station.

But a literalist among the kindergartners insists, "He couldn't. The book says he had to work as fast as he could all day. . . . It doesn't say he stopped."

Finally the teacher settles the question.

"Boys and girls," she began, speaking in her clear, distinct way. "The reason the book does not tell us how Mike Mulligan went to the bathroom is that it is not an important part of the story. The story is about digging the basement of the town hall, and that is what the book tells us."

The children are not really convinced, but that explanation has to suffice. And it strikes me that sometimes when it comes to a biblical text, especially one that really puzzles us or contradicts another passage in the Bible, we really need to ask ourselves what is and what is not an important part of the story. What is the passage trying to tell us?

That's true whether we're trying to deal with two separate creation stories, a cut-and-paste Noah's Ark narrative, the question of whether or not we can see God, or exactly which day Jesus and the disciples shared the Last Supper. Sometimes our best strategy is not to try to explain or explain away differences; it is to study the stories in their original context and to interpret them together as the people of God.

In the end, it all comes down to interpretation. When Ezra had the Torah read aloud to a people who had totally forgotten their Bible, we find, "So they read from the book, from the law of God, with interpretation. They gave the sense, so that the people understood the reading" (Neh. 8:8).

Everyone interprets the Bible. Even someone who claims to be a literalist interprets the Bible. For example, if someone claims to follow the Bible literally but eats a bacon sandwich or mixes beef and milk together in a stroganoff dish, that person is ignoring a scriptural ban and has interpreted the words of the Bible.

And if we're going to interpret the Bible, the most biblical way to do it is within a small group. The small group supports believers as we struggle to interpret the text and also provides checks and balances as the interpretations are examined and shared.

This group study will focus on some of the stories and events of the Bible that sometimes complement each other—and sometimes seem to compete. The purpose is not to call the biblical record into question, but to open the group to studying difficult issues squarely rather than simply trying to explain them away or ignoring them altogether.

The purpose is to build faith by growing to appreciate the intent and context of scripture, viewing the Bible critically and with openness to new meanings.

To this end it will not be possible to explore every aspect of a scriptural text. For instance, in the final session it would have been fun to talk about the relationship of the Galatians to the Celts, Paul's own account of his faith journey, and how crucial it is that we retain our cultural identity when we become Christians instead of trying to become one homogeneous body.

But then, a group that is committed to studying scripture together for the long term, bearing with each other patiently, intent on daily Bible reading, and is accountable to one another will get to just about everything over the long haul. This little book may never get around to explaining how Mike Mulligan went to the bathroom while working so hard on his steam shovel, but it may help such groups work together in love and patience.

Dedicated to my sisters Vivian and Victoria,
twins together, chocolate and vanilla, different as night and day.
Both/And, not Either/Or.

Frank Ramirez
Everett, Pennsylvania
2004

Resources for This Study

The New Interpreter's Study Bible, New Revised Standard Version with the Apocrypha. Abingdon Press, 2003. This study Bible includes special notes and short essays written in a clear and readable style.

Murphy, Nancey. *Reconciling Theology and Science: A Radical Reformation Perspective.* Pandora Press, 1997.

Price, Reynolds. *Three Gospels.* Simon and Schuster, 1997.

1

Creation Genesis
Genesis 1:1–2:4a and Genesis 2:4b-25

Personal Preparation

1. Consider your small group. Pray for each member of whom you are aware and for others who may yet join the group.

2. Some suggest that there are two separate creation stories in the Bible and that the first ends with Genesis 2:4a. Read Genesis 1:1–2:4a, and write out the order of creation it suggests in your journal or on a sheet of paper. Then read the "second" creation story, Genesis 2:4b-25. Once again, write out the order of creation this version suggests.

3. As you go about daily tasks, take time to note aspects of God's creation that are especially delightful in your environment. Praise God, and thank God for these things.

Suggestions for Sharing and Prayer

1. Take time for introductions, even if this is not your first meeting as a small group. Greet one another; tell a little about yourself, and fill the group in on what you have been doing recently.

2. Share news, joys, concerns, or whatever else is on your heart. During these sessions, you will be asked to pray sentence prayers in response to sharing by group members. In this context, sentence prayers are short responses such as, "Lord, we offer up to you this concern," or "Gracious God, please hear our plea," or "We give you

thanks for this good news." Sentence prayers can be very specific ("We pray for a successful surgery for _____") or more general ("We pray to you for healing"). Rather than assigning members to pray, consider simply taking turns, inviting people to offer up simple prayers as each feels led.

3. Read Psalm 104 aloud. One option is to go around the circle, with each one reading a verse and then moving to the next person. If your group is small and you all have the same Bible version, you may try reading complete sentences or even paragraphs before moving to the next person.

4. The writer of Psalm 104 lists numerous reasons to offer blessings to God. Sit in silence for a few minutes as you consider reasons you would bless the Lord. As you feel led, share your thoughts aloud.

5. Close with prayer. You might pray something like: "God of Creation, we see your hand in everything around us. You sustain us and supply us with all good things. As we gather together in your name, we ask that you grant us a measure of your love, which drew forth the entire creation of good things. Amen."

6. Sing together "Morning has broken."

Understanding

An eight-year-old asked his father, "Where did I come from?"

Deciding that the time was right, the father brought out books, charts, and diagrams and led his son through the miracles of conception and birth. The boy dutifully listened, and at the end of the lesson the father asked, "Have I answered your question?"

"Not really," the boy answered after a pause. "What I really wanted to know was where did I come from, Cleveland or Los Angeles?"

Sometimes we have the right answer to the wrong question. In the case of the creation stories in Genesis, most of the controversy centers on answers to questions the text is not asking. People get bogged down over a seven-day creation, six-thousand-year-old universe, and all those pesky dinosaur bones. For many, the question is whether the Bible presents a "true" account of creation. On this question—at least to those who phrase the problem in this fashion—everything else in the Bible stands or falls.

But seven literal days, the place of natural selection, and a young universe seem to have little to do with the questions Genesis answers. In a context of competing and flawed mythologies, Genesis seeks to answer:

- Who made the world?
- Is the world safe?
- Why is the world so good?
- Why is the world so awful?

The creation stories in Genesis are very different from nonbiblical explanations of how things came to be. Creation stories from other religions sometimes depict the gods as capricious, unreliable, or even powerless against such forces as the waters, the fates, or the stars. There is always the threat that chaos will overwhelm the creation and reduce it to rubble. The ancient Meso-Americans, for instance, feared the dissolution of creation and sought to placate the gods every half century or so with human sacrifices. The Germanic people believed that ultimately their preferred gods would be defeated by the gods of winter death.

Why Is the World So Good?

In contrast to nonbiblical stories, Genesis 1:1–2:4a presents a picture of an orderly creation that is reliable and secure. It is God who creates and controls the stars, not the stars that control the gods. Creation may be dangerous (see spiders, sharks, and tornadoes), but it is good. And humanity is an essential part of that creation. Creation is not accidental or pointless, and neither are human beings. God is why creation is good.

People want security. Children want stable households. Adults want stable jobs, incomes, and relationships. These can be difficult to guarantee. Economic downturns; changes in the way people work; broken relationships; toxic influences, such as alcohol, tobacco, drugs, and gambling, as well as genetic and environmental factors, can make stability and security difficult to attain or maintain. Life can never be made completely secure. True security lies in God, not in ourselves.

People in the ancient world feared monsters—those strange, unnatural creatures with bizarre powers that could destroy a person or the world. Even the gods were afraid of them. Some in our modern world have severe qualms about bugs, spiders, and snakes, among other things. According to the Genesis account, there are no monsters. There are marvelous creatures from the depths of the sea to the heights of the hills. Some of these are dangerous. Some are scary. But they are also wonderful. None of them are monsters. Everything is good.

We are told that God created humankind in his own image. What does this mean? For Naomi Rosenblatt, author of Wrestling with Angels, "being created in the image of God means that our spiritual potential for growth and transformation is limitless."

Does this mean that God looks like us? I doubt it. Rather, it suggests that at our best we look like God. Anthropologist Richard Leakey lost both legs in a plane crash, and while recovering he suffered from government-sponsored mob violence during a political controversy in Kenya. Yet he was able to tell reporters that what sets humanity apart is compassion. Leakey told of finding human fossils that were two million years old with broken bones that had been perfectly fused and healed. Even ancient humans cared enough to nurse the injured back to health.

In the ancient world, some people believed that only rulers who descended from gods bore the image of a god. Genesis makes it clear that the royal image is in the possession of every person, male and female. All people are made in the image of God.

When we consider the last century's legacy of genocide and horror, we may wonder if we are really stamped with God's image, but Genesis presents a picture of a humanity descended from a single set of parents. We're all related.

Why Is the World So Rotten?
The first story of creation is concerned with the whole cosmos. The second story focuses on a local setting (the Garden of

Eden), the role humans have in creation, and the risk God took by setting limits and giving people free will.

Starting with Genesis 2:4b, the act of creation is replayed from a different angle so we can see the same story in a different way. Under the guidance of God's Spirit, the two creation stories form one narrative.

In the midst of the garden are planted the tree of life and the tree of the knowledge of good and evil. Some commentators suggest that the presence of the tree of life means that humans were born mortal but had immortality within their grasp. The tree of the knowledge of good and evil, on the other hand, is more problematic. Some suggest that the knowledge in question is sexual; others suggest that after eating the fruit, Adam and Eve had their horizons widened. Some suggest that humans would have always known only good if they had not come to understand evil through their disobedience.

What is clear is that the possibility of disobedience helps the man and the woman become fully human. Without known boundaries, there can be no freedom. We cannot possibly make the free choice to obey God without an option to disobey God.

Science and Faith

I grew up in parochial schools where we learned in science class about dinosaurs living millions of years ago, followed by religious studies in which we were told about a six-day creation. It was confusing then, and I'm sure others are just as confused now about the apparent contradiction between scripture and the universe as we observe it.

Some people think that science and faith are in opposition to each other; others feel that they speak to such different spheres in our lives that they do not overlap. In her book about the relationship between science and faith, theologian Nancey Murphy writes about a hierarchy of sciences in which boundary questions should be answered by a science that is higher in the chain.

In her opinion, theology is a science that operates by the same rules as other sciences and that it completes, rather than complements, the other sciences. Theology answers those questions that go beyond science's ability to answer. Science can describe the universe as we observe it, but answers to questions about our origins ultimately depend upon our study of the Bible.

When it comes to matters of faith, science, and creation, people tend to think it's a matter of either/or. Either the Bible is literally true in describing the manner of creation, or everything in the Bible is false. But maybe sometimes the answer is both/and. Having two complementary creation stories can help us consider whether science and faith can speak with and to each other—especially if we exercise the patience to prayerfully speak with and not at one another.

Discussion and Action

1. Define the Bible. What is it? Where did it come from? How is it useful? Listen respectfully to each person's response without correcting one another or arguing. Discussion should be for the purpose of clarification or contrast, not conflict. You will be meeting together for ten sessions, so be patient. You may wish to thank God for each person in the group.

2. Why do you think God made the universe? Why did God make humans? What does it mean to be made in the image of God? Is creation over, or is it continuing? How long do you think this creation will last?

3. Look first at Genesis 1:1–2:4a and then at 2:4b-25. Do you think these are two different creation stories? If so, why do you think they are needed or are included? If not, what is the purpose of each distinct part of the story?

4. Take turns naming individuals in the larger world who are important to you. Respond to each name by saying, "Made in the image of God." Then go around again, this time naming someone by whom you are challenged or who you dislike or distrust. If anyone does not wish to say the name aloud, sit in silence for a moment and then say, "Done." Again, respond to each name with "Made in the image of God." Go around a third time, this time naming someone in your personal experience who is

very important to you. Once more, respond to each name with "Made in the image of God."

5. The scriptures suggest we are all made in the image of God. Is this something we keep forever? Is it possible to lose God's image within us?

6. The scriptures suggest that God gave humanity dominion over the rest of creation. What do you think dominion means in this regard? As a group, how might you exercise that dominion together in a positive sense this week?

7. Read Psalm 8 aloud. Close with prayer.

2

The Flood
Genesis 6:1–9:17

Personal Preparation

1. Invite a child to tell you the story of Noah's Ark and to draw or paint a picture for you to take to the session.
2. Take a moment to reflect on your memories of this story. When you were a child, what images did you have in your mind? What images come to mind now?
3. Read Genesis 6:1–9:17. In what ways do your mental images measure up to the story you find in the Bible? In what ways are they different?
4. Think about rainbows you have seen. Have some been more striking than others? Were any connected to events in your life? Take a moment to write, either in a journal or on a piece of paper, a short thought about the rainbow and God's presence in your life.

Suggestions for Sharing and Prayer

1. Greet one another, and if new people have arrived, make introductions around. Share the events of the past week. Offer sentence prayers in response to any joys and concerns shared.
2. If you have brought artwork with you, display it in the room where you are meeting. As you look at the art, share reflections from your time in Personal Preparation, including impressions you had long ago

regarding Noah's Ark or the rainbow, along with any insights you gained from children telling the story.

3. Lay out a long piece of newsprint, along with crayons and markers. Paint the story of Noah's Ark from beginning to end, putting in as many details, biblical and fanciful, as desired. Retell the story as you work together.

4. In Psalm 14, the psalmist speaks of God's frustration, and perhaps our own, with the failings of humanity. After reading the psalm, reflect on ways in which you share the frustration of the psalmist, and ways in which you have been part of the frustration.

5. Many believe that there are two flood stories in the biblical narrative, edited together side-by-side. Experts disagree on the breakdown of the two strands, but one possibility follows at the end of this session. Take time to read each version separately, singing a song (perhaps "Like Noah's weary dove") between the two readings. How well do the separate narratives work by themselves? Do you think there are really two narratives?

6. One of the central elements of the story is God's choice to save the animals. Reflect on God's creation beyond humanity, and share some of the ways in which you believe all are connected. Talk about significant connections with the natural world.

7. In this story, God's relationship with humanity is renewed and promises are made. Read Isaiah 54:7-10, and discuss the ways you have or have not felt God's promises in your life.

8. Sing "We plow the fields and scatter."

Understanding

Christian author C. S. Lewis once wrote that when you dissect a frog you might find out what's inside, but one thing is certain— you won't have a frog anymore.

He made the point while commenting on the efforts by some to dissect literature, both sacred and secular. It's important to identify source material, different strands of oral tradition, and layers of composition, but it's a mistake to think that doing so somehow makes you superior to the work you are studying.

The story of Noah's Ark is a very good example. Two different creation stories, each with a different aim, open the book of Genesis. By incorporating both versions of the beginning, the Bible presents a complete picture of the universe as we find it. The versions lay side-by-side and can be compared fairly easily.

Similarly, some believe there are two flood narratives in Genesis from two different sources, each with something to teach and to contribute to the story as a whole as it is presented in the Bible. Review these two stories as they appear at the end of this session. Though each may stand alone, it is important to remember that the truth of the narrative lies in its meaning as presented in the Bible, not in taking it apart to look inside at the guts.

Sometimes we pay more attention to the exact nature of the flood and how it was experienced by humanity. As with creation, if we get bogged down in the actual details, we'll lose sight of the story's meaning, which is the same whether we believe the flood covered every inch of the earth's surface, or whether it was limited to the world as known by humanity at that time. What matters is how the Bible handles what seems to have been a story shared by most cultures in the ancient world.

The story of a world-destroying flood is a common theme in mythology. Some suggest that a deluge occurring around the year 2900 B.C., may have been the source for these stories. In the Sumerian epic, for instance, the gods decide to destroy humanity because they are making too much noise and are too fertile. But the gods are shocked by the power of the flood they loosed and are unable to control it. One god rebels, breaks ranks, and saves a human being against the will of all the other gods.

The biblical account stands in marked contrast to the other stories because Genesis portrays a God in total control. God's decision to destroy humanity is not capricious. God reacts to humanity's depravity. Throughout the process, God controls the waters, which in the ancient world were a symbol of chaos and destruction, and God intends from the beginning to save a remnant of the human family along with representatives of the animal kingdom, in order to renew the earth.

Double Vision

About thirty years ago I took two different colored highlighters and marked up the first eleven chapters in Genesis to indicate what one expert thought was the division between the two different traditions. If you try to do something similar based on these suggestions, you will find that, for the most part, either version presents pretty much the same picture. God reacts to the depravity of humanity with grief over the creation and resolves to wipe the earth clean. However, Noah's righteousness causes God to choose to preserve him and his family against the flood. The terrible power of the waters is loosed, but God is in control. When God is ready, the waters are shut off, and they recede according to God's plan. Once humanity is reunited with the land, God promises never again to flood the earth. There is a new beginning.

What complicates the study of this passage is that there are not only two flood narratives, but they are woven together so well that experts cannot agree on exactly where one begins and the other leaves off.

However, the signs of their existence are pretty clear. Sometimes God is referred to by name as Yahweh, and other times by a Hebrew word for God, *Elohim.* Generally, the use of two such terms is a sign that different authors are involved. In this story, the names the authors use for God are the names given to their versions of the story.

In the Yahweh account, the rain falls for forty days and forty nights (see 7:4, 12, 17; 8:6), and seven pairs of clean animals are brought into the ark (7:2-3) for a sacrifice that takes place afterwards (8:20).

In the Elohist version, the flood is caused by a basic disintegration of the universe (7:11; 8:2) and the flood lasts a year (7:11, 24; 8:3b, 4-5, 13-14) and only one pair of animals is brought onto the ark (6:19-20) since no sacrifice is offered afterwards.

There are some interesting differences. The Yahwist presents a God who shares many of our human qualities. This author focuses on the blessing given to God's people and the promise given by God for land.

The Elohist source sees history as a series of covenants. The first is with Noah, the second is with Abraham, and the third is with Israel at Mt. Sinai.

The story of Noah's Ark is one of the most popular in scripture. Kids love books about the ark. Plays and musicals have been written about it. It is a popular theme for paintings, sculptures, and other forms of art.

In the early years when Christianity was illegal, Noah was second only to Jonah as the most popular motif for art. These early artworks generally depict Noah as a tiny figure in a box carried upon the waves. This story provided assurance of salvation from the chaos of the world around us through the waters of baptism.

As an adult, my reflection on this story includes wondering what humanity could have done that was so terrible that a merciful and loving God would want to destroy them. But we, of all people, should not be surprised. The past century includes plenty of examples of the horrors people are willing to inflict on others.

In the end, this is a story of hope and promise—and of a covenant with all humanity. Jewish authorities recognized that this covenant extended beyond the faith community to embrace everyone. Jewish Christians meeting with the Apostle Paul in Jerusalem around the year A.D. 48 (described in Acts 15) decided there was no need for the Gentile converts to follow their understanding of Hebrew scriptures, but instead they should follow what they called the Code of Noah. By that they meant that all humanity understands basic morality and these laws are binding upon everyone whether they've received a revelation or not.

Back to the dissected frog analogy—this sort of analysis can only tell us so much. It might be useful knowledge, but it does not give us power over the text. We received the text as it is edited, and that is God's word, regardless of how it came here. Faced with a question of either/or, the biblical writer chose both/and, pulling from both accounts.

Discussion and Action

1. How does the flood story help us grow in our faith and in our understanding of who God is and how God acts in the world?

2. What does each version leave us with as far as a lesson about our relationship with God? What does each say about the nature of God and of humanity?

3. Are we living in a "secure" universe, or is creation under the threat of annihilation? Give examples to support your answer. Do our actions have consequences, and if so, can these consequences be felt with regard to the possibilities of global warming, depletion of resources, and the exploitation of natural resources?

4. In Bill Moyers' book *Genesis: A Living Conversation,* theologian Karen Armstrong mentions that she can't recall the rainbow without calling to mind the animals, the mud, and the bloated bodies of all those who died in the flood. But Samuel Proctor, an African-American minister, holds onto the hope in the story. Calling to mind the long march of blacks toward equality in American society, he says, "I can't turn loose this story of Noah and the flood because, after all of the devastation and the bloated bodies, there's the rainbow and the cloud. I'm not going to live without that kind of hope, you see?" Where do you find yourselves as individuals and as a group, in this discussion? Is this a discussion you had even considered? What constitutes hope in your life? When, if ever, are you without hope?

5. Together tell the story of Noah's Ark from the viewpoint of someone outside the ark, perhaps that of a child. Are there some who are being left behind in your community or your world? In what ways can the group work together to reach out to those people?

Elohist Flood Story
Genesis 6:9-22; 7:6, 8-9, 11, 13-16a, 18-21, 24;
8:1-2a, 3b-5, 7, 13a, 14-19; 9:1-17

These are the descendants of Noah. Noah was a righteous man, blameless in his generation; Noah walked with God. And Noah had three sons, Shem, Ham, and Japheth. Now the earth was corrupt in God's sight, and the earth was filled with violence. And God saw that the earth was corrupt; for all flesh had corrupted its ways upon the earth.

And God said to Noah, "I have determined to make an end of all flesh, for the earth is filled with violence because of them; now I am going to destroy them along with the earth. Make yourself an ark of cypress wood; make rooms in the ark, and cover it inside and out with pitch. This is how you are to make it: the length of the ark three hundred cubits, its width fifty cubits, and its height thirty cubits. Make a roof for the ark, and finish it to a cubit above; and put the door of the ark in its side; make it with lower, second, and third decks. For my part, I am going to bring a flood of waters on the earth, to destroy from under heaven all flesh in which is the breath of life; everything that is on the earth shall die. But I will establish my covenant with you; and you shall come into the ark, you, your sons, your wife, and your sons' wives with you. And of every living thing, of all flesh, you shall bring two of every kind into the ark, to keep them alive with you; they shall be male and female. Of the birds according to their kinds, and of the animals according to their kinds, of every creeping thing of the ground according to its kind, two of every kind shall come in to you, to keep them alive. Also take with you every kind of food that is eaten, and store it up; and it shall serve as food for you and for them."

Noah did this; he did all that God commanded him. Noah was six hundred years old when the flood of waters came on the earth. Of clean animals, and of animals that are not clean, and of birds, and of everything that creeps on the ground, two and two, male and female, went into the ark with Noah, as God had commanded Noah.

In the six hundredth year of Noah's life, in the second month, on the seventeenth day of the month, on that day all the fountains of the great deep burst forth, and the windows of the heavens were opened.

On the very same day Noah with his sons, Shem and Ham and Japheth, and Noah's wife and the three wives of his sons entered the ark, they and every wild animal of every kind, and all domestic animals of every kind, and every creeping thing that creeps on the earth, and every bird of every kind—every bird, every winged creature. They went into the ark with Noah, two and two of all flesh in which there was the breath of life. And those that entered, male and female of all flesh, went in as God had commanded him; the waters swelled and increased greatly on the earth; and the ark floated on the face of the waters. The waters swelled so mightily on the earth that all the high mountains under the whole heaven were covered; the waters swelled above the mountains, covering them fifteen cubits deep.

And all flesh died that moved on the earth, birds, domestic animals, wild animals, all swarming creatures that swarm on the earth, and all human beings. And the waters swelled on the earth for one hundred fifty days.

But God remembered Noah and all the wild animals and all the domestic animals that were with him in the ark. And God made a wind blow over the earth, and the waters subsided; the fountains of the deep and the windows of the heavens were closed. At the end of one hundred fifty days the waters had abated; and in the seventh month, on the seventeenth day of the month, the ark came to rest on the mountains of Ararat. The waters continued to abate until the tenth month; in the tenth month, on the first day of the month, the tops of the mountains appeared.

And [Noah] sent out the raven; and it went to and fro until the waters were dried up from the earth.

In the six hundred first year, in the first month, the first day of the month, the waters were dried up from the earth. In the second month, on the twenty-seventh day of the month, the earth was dry.

Then God said to Noah, "Go out of the ark, you and your wife, and your sons and your sons' wives with you. Bring out with you every living thing that is with you of all flesh—birds and animals and every creeping thing that creeps on the earth— so that they may abound on the earth, and be fruitful and multiply on the earth." So Noah went out with his sons and his wife and his sons' wives. And every animal, every creeping thing, and every bird, everything that moves on the earth, went out of the ark by families.

God blessed Noah and his sons, and said to them, "Be fruitful and multiply, and fill the earth. The fear and dread of you shall rest on every animal of the earth, and on every bird of the air, on everything that creeps on the ground, and on all the fish of the sea; into your hand they are delivered. Every moving thing that lives shall be food for you; and just as I gave you the green plants, I give you everything. Only, you shall not eat flesh with its life, that is, its blood. For your own lifeblood I will surely require a reckoning: from every animal I will require it and from human beings, each one for the blood of another, I will require a reckoning for human life. Whoever sheds the blood of a human, by a human shall that person's blood be shed; for in his own image God made humankind. And you, be fruitful and multiply, abound on the earth and multiply in it."

Then God said to Noah and to his sons with him, "As for me, I am establishing my covenant with you and your descendants after you, and with every living creature that is with you, the birds, the domestic animals, and every animal of the earth with you, as many as came out of the ark. I establish my covenant with you, that never again shall all flesh be cut off by the waters of a flood, and never again shall there be a flood to destroy the earth."

God said, "This is the sign of the covenant that I make between me and you and every living creature that is with you, for all future generations: I have set my bow in the clouds, and it shall be a sign of the covenant between me and the earth. When I bring clouds over the earth and the bow is seen in the clouds, I will remember my covenant that is between me and you and every living creature of all flesh; and the waters shall never again become a flood to destroy all flesh. When the bow is in the clouds, I will see it and remember the everlasting covenant between God and every living creature of all flesh that is on the earth."

God said to Noah, "This is the sign of the covenant that I have established between me and all flesh that is on the earth."

Yahwist Flood Story
Genesis 6:1-8; 7:1-5, 7, 10, 12, 16b-17, 22-23;
8:2b-3a, 6, 8-12, 13b, 20-22

When people began to multiply on the face of the ground, and daughters were born to them, the sons of God saw that they were fair; and they took wives for themselves of all that they chose. Then the LORD said, "My spirit shall not abide in mortals forever, for they are flesh; their days shall be one hundred twenty years."

The Nephilim were on the earth in those days—and also afterward—when the sons of God went in to the daughters of humans, who bore children to them. These were the heroes that were of old, warriors of renown. The LORD saw that the wickedness of humankind was great in the earth, and that every inclination of the thoughts of their hearts was only evil continually.

And the LORD was sorry that he had made humankind on the earth, and it grieved him to his heart. So the LORD said, "I will blot out from the earth the human beings I have created—people together with animals and creeping things and birds of the air, for I am sorry that I have made them."

But Noah found favor in the sight of the LORD.

Then the LORD said to Noah, "Go into the ark, you and all your household, for I have seen that you alone are righteous before me in this generation. Take with you seven pairs of all clean animals, the male and its mate; and a pair of the animals that are not clean, the male and its mate; and seven pairs of the birds of the air also, male and female, to keep their kind alive on the face of all the earth. For in seven days I will send rain on the earth for forty days and forty nights; and every living thing that I have made I will blot out from the face of the ground."

And Noah did all that the LORD had commanded him.

And Noah with his sons and his wife and his sons' wives went into the ark to escape the waters of the flood. And after seven days the waters of the flood came on the earth.

The rain fell on the earth forty days and forty nights. And the LORD shut him in. The flood continued forty days on the earth; and the waters increased, and bore up the ark, and it rose high above the earth. Everything on dry land in whose nostrils was the breath of life died. He blotted out every living thing that was on the face of the ground, human beings and animals and creeping things and birds of the air; they were blotted out from the earth. Only Noah was left, and those that were with him in the ark.

The rain from the heavens was restrained, and the waters gradually receded from the earth.

At the end of forty days Noah opened the window of the ark that he had made. Then he sent out the dove from him, to see if the waters had subsided from the face of the ground; but the dove found no place to set its foot, and it returned to him to the ark, for the waters were still on the face of the whole earth. So he put out his hand and took it and brought it into the ark with him. He waited another seven days, and again he sent out the dove from the ark; and the dove came back to him in the evening, and there in its beak was a freshly plucked olive leaf; so Noah knew that the waters had subsided from the earth. Then he waited another seven days, and sent out the dove; and it did not return to him any more. And Noah removed the covering of the ark, and looked, and saw that the face of the ground was drying.

Then Noah built an altar to the LORD, and took of every clean animal and of every clean bird, and offered burnt offerings on the altar.

And when the LORD smelled the pleasing odor, the LORD said in his heart, "I will never again curse the ground because of humankind, for the inclination of the human heart is evil from youth; nor will I ever again destroy every living creature as I have done. As long as the earth endures, seedtime and harvest, cold and heat, summer and winter, day and night, shall not cease."

3

Which Ten Commandments?
Exodus 20:1-17 and Deuteronomy 5:6-21

Personal Preparation

1. Without looking at your Bible, take time to write out the Ten Commandments. Now look up both Exodus 20:1-17 and Deuteronomy 5:6-21 and compare these texts with your list.

2. Perform an internet search on the Ten Commandments. What sorts of things come up? Do they seem to be devotional in nature? Are they concerned with news events?

3. Divide the Ten Commandments into those commands you think apply to our relationship with God and those you think apply to our relationships with others. Consider ways in which you have served both God and others.

4. What rules, spoken or unspoken, does your study group observe? Do you believe it is a safe place to speak, to pray, to share?

Suggestions for Sharing and Prayer

1. Greet one another with the words "The peace of our blessed Lord be with you," and respond by answering, "We share this selfsame peace."

2. Take time to share joys and concerns, and pray for one another out loud or silently.

3. Write the words LAW, LIFE, and LOVE on newsprint or a chalkboard. Together, brainstorm positive words about God, law, relationship, and prayer that begin with the

letters that comprise these words. List these words under the letters you have printed out.

4. Open your Bibles to Psalm 119, which is a celebration of God's law. This psalm consists of twenty-four stanzas of eight lines. The lines of each stanza begin with the same letter in Hebrew, the language in which the Psalms were originally written, and are part of a complex poem praising God for caring enough to give guidance. Read the psalm as a group, with each member praying a stanza as you move around the circle.

5. Sing the praise chorus "Thy Word."

6. Read Jeremiah 31:31-33 in unison. Consider together ways in which the new covenant written on our hearts helps us to keep God's law—with or without a written copy.

7. Close by recalling the joys and concerns shared at the beginning of the session. Stand or sit in a circle and join hands to pray again for one another. Begin with the group leader praying for the person on his or her left. After praying aloud or silently, squeeze the hand of the group member to the left. That person may either pray aloud for the person on his or her left, or squeeze the next hand and so on, until the prayer comes back to the group leader, who will conclude by leading in the Lord's Prayer.

Understanding

When I lived near Elkhart, Indiana, there was a protracted legal battle over a display of the Ten Commandments in front of the county courthouse. To say it was a hot button issue would be putting it mildly. People on both sides of the issue were more than glad to spar in public, leading to a lot of verbal fireworks. The "letters to the editor" columns of the local papers were filled with invective as people sought to save western civilization from collapse.

Meanwhile, money was poured down a black hole to protect or remove the monument, while many other pressing issues were ignored. The bills mounted. In the end, folks simply decided that the battle wasn't worth it and the monument was removed to a nearby plot of private land.

There is a lot of attention given nowadays to "protecting" the Ten Commandments. In my opinion there ought to be more attention given to reading them, because what they demand is not protection, but observance.

They demand observance.

One of the questions rarely asked in a monument controversy is, "Which version—Jewish, Catholic/Lutheran, or mainline Protestant—do you want to display?" Among people of faith, there are at least three different ways to number the Ten Commandments. Technically, the Hebrew Bible calls them the Ten Words, but some rabbis found thirteen commandments in these 146 Hebrew words.

Typically, mainline Protestants divide the commandments into four that govern our relationship with God and six governing our relationships with humanity, shortened in this manner:

> I am the Lord your God, you shall have no other gods before me.
> You shall not make for yourself an idol.
> You shall not make wrongful use of the name of the LORD your God.
> Remember the sabbath day, and keep it holy.
> Honor your father and your mother.
> You shall not murder.
> You shall not commit adultery.
> You shall not steal.
> You shall not bear false witness against your neighbor.
> You shall not covet your neighbor's goods.

Typically, Catholics and some other Christians will combine the first and second commandment and separate the tenth into two, forbidding men to covet a neighbor's wife and to refrain from coveting a neighbor's goods. In some Jewish traditions, the first phrase, "I am the Lord your God," is the first commandment, and the injunctions against other gods and idols are combined into one.

If you have taken the time before this session to read the Ten Commandments as found in both Exodus and Deuteronomy, you will see that while commandments six through nine are every bit as terse as they appear above, the others are more complex.

Life and Limb

Many years ago I was driving swiftly across Kansas on a two-lane highway—until I came upon a temporary sign that simply told me to be careful, because unmarked trucks were carrying nuclear weapons.

I was more careful.

The Ten Commandments are warnings that invite us to change our behavior for the sake of life. While most of the laws contained in the Torah (the first five books of the Bible) are casuistic (that is, if you do such and such, the result will be so and so), there are no ifs, ands, or buts about the Ten Commandments. They are phrased in second person singular so that each of us takes them personally, but they are addressed to God's people corporately so we obey them together.

First and foremost, we must acknowledge God as Lord and accept no substitutes. God forbids the making of idols as well as the misuse of the divine name. God forbids concrete actions such as murder, adultery, theft, and lying in court, as well as the destructive thoughts that end in jealousy or coveting.

The commandments remind us that God has a history with us. God is the one who released the people from their bondage in Egypt. God has a claim upon the people for all time.

The commandments aimed toward the divine and those aimed toward humanity find their intersection in sabbath rest and in honoring one's parents: "so that your days may be long in the land that the LORD your God is giving you" (Exod. 20:12). It's important to note that individuals who honor their parents might still die young, while those who ignore or abuse their parents might live to a ripe old age, but overall the society will be healthier when honor is given to previous generations. When society breaks down, all of us suffer.

A Law of Tolerance

The real intersection between God and humanity is found in the sabbath. It is in this commandment that we see the greatest difference between the versions in Exodus and Deuteronomy. It is good to remember that in the case of the former, the commandments are being delivered to a people in the desert, while the latter recalls Moses' farewell speech to the people before they enter into the Promised Land without him.

One significant difference lies in the reason for keeping the sabbath. The Exodus text points backward to creation as one reason for the sabbath. We are called to imitate God in taking life-giving rest. The Deuteronomic text points to God freeing the people from slavery in Egypt. Both versions extend the blessing to everyone, including animals. The Exodus passage explains its origin. The Deuteronomy scripture explains a motive for observing it.

In a sense, this whole seven-day cycle is counter-intuitive. Neither the lunar month nor the solar year is divisible by seven, so we can't say the sabbath was the natural result of observing nature. To those who are driven by worldly motivations, the sabbath is a great waste. The Roman Seneca, who died in A.D. 65, said, "To spend every seventh day without doing anything means to lose a seventh part of life, besides suffering loss in pressing matters from such idleness."

But this is a day of joy and peace. Note that the commandment doesn't even demand worship—only rest. It is to be a day, as one author put it, "to celebrate time rather than space." Honoring God by honoring the sabbath refreshes and renews humanity.

Nahum M. Sarna wrote that "human liberty is immeasurably enhanced, human equality is strengthened, and the cause of social justice is promoted by legislating the inalienable right of every human being, irrespective of social class, and of draft animals as well, to twenty-four hours of complete rest every seven days."

More than anywhere else in the Torah, the laws of Deuteronomy are aimed to benefit the poor and disadvantaged, including orphans, widows, debtors, escaped slaves, resident aliens—everyone. And these are the groups toward whom Jesus aimed his ministry as well.

There are those who chafe against any sort of regulation and believe that their freedoms are denied by even the simplest of rules. They claim they want no society, just unadulterated freedom. But in recent years we have seen a number of situations in various countries where the social compact has totally broken down, where slaughter and genocide proceeded unchecked, where lack of law led not to freedom but to death.

In our own society, we have seen in a milder sense how the breakdown of boundaries in civil discourse leads to a kind of societal death. Two different ways of thinking and interpreting the world exist side by side in a poisoned atmosphere without any way of bridging the gap—if there is even any desire to bridge the gap. In this lack of civil discourse, some seize upon issues such as the public display of the Ten Commandments to demonize their opposition, and in doing so they appear to be using God for personal gain. I think God is far more interested in us working for the kingdom than engaging in legal battles over words that were meant to be obeyed rather than merely displayed.

Discussion and Action

1. How are we shaped by the Ten Commandments in our congregational settings? How much attention do we pay to them? Do we regard them as "old and irrelevant" or "current and relevant"?

2. What evidence shows us how these commandments are played out in the life of our faith community? What are ways in which we could make them more prominent in our witness to the world? How might this be done without adding to the polarization in society generated by debates over the Ten Commandments?

3. Consider whether your study group is a safe place to share and to pray together. If so, what makes it safe? Recognize that if someone doesn't consider your group a safe place, they aren't likely to mention it to the group. It might be helpful to think more broadly about what

boundaries are necessary for a safe place to be established. Are such boundaries usually spoken or unspoken? How does this apply to your study group?

4. Read together the Ten Commandments from Exodus 20 and Deuteronomy 5. What is the significance of including the Ten Commandments in two different books? Which commandment do you think is most important? Which one is least important? Why? Which are the hardest and the easiest to follow?

5. In your estimation, which commandment is ignored most in the world? Which is observed by the most number of people? Why do you think this might be so?

6. Read Mark 12:28-34 aloud. When Jesus was challenged to name the most important commandment, he quoted Leviticus 19:18 and Deuteronomy 6:4. Which of the Ten Commandments are covered under these two commandments? Are there any that could be ignored? Does Jesus' answer simplify or complicate things? What obligations and boundaries are created by his words?

4

Seeing and Not Seeing God
Exodus 24:9-11 and Exodus 33:7-23

Personal Preparation

1. Invite a child to draw a picture of God. Give no instructions or ideas, and allow the child to choose the medium. Bring this artwork to the session.
2. Ask your friends and members of your family to describe or draw God. Consider the images of God that have been both helpful and unhelpful for you. Bring your notes to the session.
3. Reflect on instances in your past or present when God was especially present. Write a paragraph on the topic "The God I Cannot See."
4. Find a quiet place. Close your eyes and breathe deeply. Try to remove every image, including your images of God, from your mind. If you feel led, pray.

Suggestions for Sharing and Prayer

1. Gather together by singing "In the rifted rock I'm resting." As a group, read Exodus 33:7-23 aloud. Invite someone to read the words of Moses, another God's words, and a third person to be the narrator (reading everything else).
2. Take time now to share about your encounters with God from your personal preparation (3). What was visible in the encounter? What was invisible? Was God's presence apparent at the time or only afterwards? Did others

share in this experience with you, or were you alone with God? If some have taken time to write a paragraph on "The God I Cannot See," share them now.

3. Display the children's pictures (Personal Preparation 1) on a bulletin board or wall where you can all walk around and appreciate the creations.

4. If you took time to ask your adult friends to describe or draw God (Personal Preparation 2), share these observations as well. What, if anything, do the adult and child observations have in common? What differences do you find in the descriptions? How are our images of God formed? What might account for the ways in which our images of God change over time?

5. Gather quietly in a circle, taking enough time to become comfortable with the silence. After a time, invite prayers for God's presence to be revealed in the lives of group members. Encourage each person, as they feel led, to pray for someone else in the group by name. As the leader, make sure all members have been prayed for, then bring the prayer to a close as you see fit.

6. Sing together "A wonderful Savior is Jesus my Lord." Close with a unison reading of Exodus 24:9-11.

Understanding

In high school I took a Bible as Literature course. One day the teacher mentioned a new translation of the Torah, the first five books of the Bible. I asked my father for a copy, and the book soon made its appearance.

I would have been very reluctant to mark up a Bible, but somehow this book, with cloth binding and paper cover, looked so much like a regular book that I didn't have the slightest problem taking a blue highlighter and marking up every passage that intrigued me.

There was a lot I found fascinating, from the odd account of the Sons of God and the Daughters of Men in Genesis 6:1-4, through the talking donkey in Numbers, and a copper serpent that healed.

More than thirty years have gone by since I marked up that book. Recently I preached a series of sermons on those passages. One of the sermons was on the two scriptures from Exodus for this session. In the first passage, Moses and the elders climb up the mountain and see God and live. In the second, God makes it clear that no one can see God and live.

Okay. Which is it?

The Old Testament seems to suggest that two equal and opposite things are true. You cannot see God and live. You can see God and live.

Can you see God? For something that's supposed to be impossible, it happens more than we guess in the scriptures.

Prior to the birth of their son Samson, Manoah and his wife were certain they had been in the presence of God. Manoah despairs and says aloud, "We shall surely die, for we have seen God" (Judg. 13:22). His wife is far more practical. She points out that if God had intended to kill them he'd have done it already.

Isaiah was pretty sure he was a goner when he found himself in the heavenly court. He cries out, "Woe is me! I am lost, for I am a man of unclean lips, and I live among a people of unclean lips; yet my eyes have seen the King, the LORD of hosts!" (Isa. 6:5). But the experience was not killing, but cleansing.

In Exodus 3:6, Moses encounters God through the burning bush. Afraid to look at God, he hides his face. Abraham and Sarah receive three visitors in the desert, and one of them seems awfully divine. He shares with Abraham the fate of Sodom and Gomorrah and is willing to bargain about their destruction.

Jacob wrestles with a figure the text calls "a man," but when he limps away from the encounter he calls the place Peniel, which means "the face of God," because, in his words, he has looked on the face of God and yet lives.

One of the most striking divine encounters takes place in Joshua 5:13-15. Prior to the battle of Jericho, the commander of the army of the Lord visits Joshua. Many commentators think that the commander of the army of the Lord has to be, well, the Lord of Hosts.

Joshua asks, "Are you one of us, or one of our adversaries?" (5:14). As soon as the man identifies himself, Joshua refers to him as "my Lord" and asks for instruction. The reply comes, "Remove the sandals from your feet, for the place where you stand is holy" (5:15). Joshua complies.

From these passages it is clear that no one can see God and be left unchanged. These passages are scattered among different books of the Bible and may be explained as different traditions. But what are we to do with two passages from the same book, Exodus, that seem to suggest opposite things?

In Exodus 24:9-11, Moses leads the elders up the mountain and they see God. The only report they bring back is about the color of the floor, but God "did not lay his hand on the chief men of the people of Israel." In other words, he didn't kill them.

In Exodus 33:7-13, Moses asks that God make clear the divine plan for the people and asks to see God's glory. God grants the request, but adds, "You cannot see my face; for no one shall see me and live" (33:20). Moses is allowed to see only God's back.

So which is it? Do we see God or not? To what extent does grace allow us to make sense of an apparent contradiction?

Perhaps the problem is that the line between God and angels is much thinner in the Old Testament. An angel is understood in some of the older passages to be a manifestation of God, not an individual being, as we have come to think of angels.

And it's not clear what people see when they encounter God. Isaiah saw the hem of God's garment. Moses and the elders saw the floor on which God was standing. In Revelation there's a report on the throne of God, but not on God sitting on the throne. But that may be sidestepping the issue.

Perhaps the difficulty comes in trying to clear up the differences between the two passages and, therefore, to clarify God. No one has penetrated the mystery of who God is. Is it possible for us to state categorically how the God experience, or experiencing God, works? The Lord is beyond knowing, boxing, labeling, or controlling. God is God.

Despite that, many people want to somehow modify or explain away apparent discrepancies. Since they believe the Bible is perfect—according to their standards of perfection—there can't be any errors, as they understand errors.

What I like best about these passages is that it is not possible to control or contain God. Every time we think we know something ("No one can see God and live"), it turns out we don't know anything. God is perfect and the Bible is perfect.

But not by our standards.

Returning to the first Exodus passage, one of the more compelling aspects of the story is that Moses and the elders ate and drank in God's presence. They had come to the table of the Lord.

They eat and drink. They don't say anything. They don't die. It should have killed them; it should have been too much. But they come to a place where they, and we, can meet God safely. Thanks to the ordinance of communion, we can see God and live. Or as Hebrews puts it (deliberately calling to mind the Book of Exodus): "You have not come to something that can be touched, a blazing fire, and darkness, and gloom, and a tempest. . . . But you have come to Mount Zion and to the city of the living God, the heavenly Jerusalem . . . and to Jesus, the mediator of a new covenant" (Heb.12:18, 22a, 24a).

That's the difference God makes through Jesus. The disciples on the road to Emmaus walked with the Risen Lord, broke bread and ate with God, and lived. In communion we come into God's presence, die to ourselves, and live forever.

There are limits to the presence, but they are God's limits. God is self-giving; God decides who shall see and live. It is dangerous to call down God; it could kill you. That's why God warned Moses. Sometimes we need to do it anyway. We can see God and live.

God's control of the encounter is crucial. There is no magic involved. We do not command God to come into our presence. We are invited.

In our time, political parties and Christian factions seek to control God by proclaiming exactly what God can or cannot do, will or will not do, will sanction or will condemn. That's more than I know, and I've been marking up Bibles for decades. God isn't in anyone's hip pocket. Yet that's the kind of God a lot of people seem to want—a pocket God.

A pocket God rests out of the way in a convenient place until that person—politician, preacher, parent—needs God for back-up. Then the pocket God is brought out for a convenient verse or two, wriggled around like a puppet to scare people, and put back in the pocket.

This is nothing short of idolatry.

Rather than seeking to explain everything, believers might respond as Moses did in both passages—approach God with awe and respect, as a servant and not as a master.

Remember Joshua's encounter with God? Joshua quickly realizes the question is not whether God is on our side, but whether we are on God's side. God's side is not convenient or practical; it does not fit into any particular ideology or "ism." Our response in the presence of God is either to take off our shoes for we are on holy ground, or to rejoice when we recognize the presence of God in ourselves. As 1 John 4:12 says: "No one has ever seen God; if we love one another, God lives in us, and his love is perfected in us."

Discussion and Action

1. Who is God? Work together as a group to come up with an answer to this question. Discuss whether we can ever truly know or define God.
2. Share about times when you felt you were in the presence of what you might describe as God or an angel. If you don't have a personal experience to share, reflect on stories others have told you or on the scripture texts noted by the author. What are common threads in these stories? What is unique about each encounter?
3. Talk about the visible, yet invisible, nature of God. Why is God invisible? How has God been made visible to you?
4. What does it mean for the church to be "the face of God" to the world? In what ways does the church make God

visible? How do people react to the God they see through the church?

5. Find a short-term (or long-term) project the group might undertake to display the love of God in the world. Make an action plan for getting it started.

6. In popcorn fashion, call out words or phrases describing God. Write them on a chalkboard or newsprint. Drawing from this list, work together to write a description of God. If your group is large, divide into pairs or triads to write your descriptions; then share them with one another.

7. End with one person reading John 1:1-18 aloud, followed by silent reflection and prayer. After a time, reread the final verse in unison. Close by singing "How great thou art."

5

An Unchanging God?
Malachi 3:6 and Exodus 32:1-14

Personal Preparation

1. Take either a blank piece of paper or a page from your journal. One at a time, copy out by hand the two different biblical texts. Below each one write a one-sentence description about God that you glean from that passage.
2. Reflect on how your relationships have changed over the past year, for good or ill. Take a moment to pray for each person who comes to mind.
3. What is the greatest change you have witnessed in your lifetime, public or personal? What has remained solidly the same in your life?

Suggestions for Sharing and Prayer

1. As you gather, share significant moments from the past week with each other. With each moment that is shared, pray together in response, "For this too, we thank you, Lord. For this too, we pray."
2. Read aloud Lamentations 3:19-24. Sing one stanza of "Great is thy faithfulness."
3. For each of the next three questions, it might be helpful to takes notes or create timelines to reflect the changes and growth you've experienced. First, relate how your experiences of worship have changed over the years. What significant ways of worshiping have remained the

same? What does it mean if not much has changed? Have the changes all been for the better or is it a mixed bag?

4. Reflect as well on the ways you have changed over the years. How has what you bring to worship changed? What about you has stayed the same? Have your attitudes about worship or your expectations of worship changed, or have they stayed the same? What are your growing edges or nagging challenges?

5. Finally, reflect on how your views of God have changed over the years and on ways in which your perceptions of God have remained the same.

6. Create a comfortable space for prayer. Take turns reading from Psalm 106 and praying one-sentence prayers about the verses. The prayer could be a reflection on the verse, a petition, rephrasing, repetition, or whatever you are led to share. There are forty-eight verses in the psalm, so if time is an issue, consider grouping verses together (such as in the NRSV). After someone reads, the person next to them prays. The person who prayed then reads the next verse(s) and the person beside them prays, and so on.

7. Close by singing all verses of "Great is thy faithfulness."

Understanding

When the kids were growing up, we told them unequivocally to never, ever touch the stove. No ifs, ands, or buts. You can't touch the stove. You may never touch the stove. All three kids are now adults. They're all great cooks. They touch the stove. At some point we reversed ourselves when the relationship suited, and the rule changed.

Also, we changed as parents. Our children grew. We grew. As parents we changed our rules. What didn't change was our love and devotion.

I tell this story because I'm trying to get a handle on what seems to be a real biblical contradiction.

God doesn't change. God changes. It can't be both, right?

"For I the LORD do not change" (Mal. 3:6).

"God is not a human being, that he should lie, or a mortal, that he should change his mind" (Num. 23:19).

"Moreover the Glory of Israel will not recant or change his mind; for he is not a mortal, that he should change his mind" (1 Sam. 15:29).

And just so you don't think this is an Old Testament thing, here is James 1:17: "Every generous act of giving, with every perfect gift, is from above, coming down from the Father of lights, with whom there is no variation or shadow due to change."

But countering that is the passage from Exodus 32:1-14, in which the people anger God one time too many. God resolves to destroy the people, but Moses argues with God, going so far as to suggest that the move will make God look bad. "And the LORD changed his mind about the disaster that he planned to bring on his people" (Exod. 32:14).

This happens a lot.

"But when the angel stretched out his hand toward Jerusalem to destroy it, the LORD relented concerning the evil, and said to the angel who was bringing destruction among the people, 'It is enough; now stay your hand' " (2 Sam. 24:16).

"But if that nation, concerning which I have spoken, turns from its evil, I will change my mind about the disaster that I intended to bring on it" (Jer. 18:8).

"When God saw what they did, how they turned from their evil ways, God changed his mind about the calamity that he had said he would bring upon them; and he did not do it" (Jonah 3:10).

And in 2 Kings 20:1-6, it only takes some weeping for God's mind to change about King Hezekiah's death. God grants fifteen more years of life, and even when Hezekiah betrays God by showing the treasuries to the Babylonian spies, God doesn't rescind the fifteen years.

On the one hand, scripture portrays a God who is rock solid, unchanging, one who knows us before we are born. On the other hand, we run into scriptures such as the Exodus passage where Moses was able to talk God out of destroying people because it will make God look bad!

There's also the passage from Genesis 18:23-32 where Abraham is able to bargain with God, getting God to promise that if at least ten righteous people are found in the cities of the plain then Sodom and Gomorrah will not be destroyed.

Which is it? Either A or B? Both A and B? Can the contradictions be resolved? Can we live with both alternatives? Should any picture of God be simple?

Maybe there's another way of looking at things. Proof-texting can be used to support both positions, but a relationship with God needs no proof.

The hymn "Great is thy faithfulness" suggests that God doesn't change ("There is no shadow of turning with thee"). But what is really unchanging, the hymn suggests, is "Thy compassions, they fail not." That's the relationship one of my favorite texts, Lamentations 3:19-24, upon which the hymn is based, speaks about: "The steadfast love of the LORD never ceases, his mercies never come to an end; they are new every morning; great is your faithfulness" (22-23).

Previously, I only quoted half of the passage from Malachi 3:6. The full verse reads: "For I the LORD do not change; therefore you, O children of Jacob, have not perished." God's unchanging relationship preserves and protects us, and that is what causes God to relent.

In 2 Timothy 2:11-13 we read this amazing passage: "The saying is sure: If we have died with him, we will also live with him; if we endure, we will also reign with him; if we deny him, he will also deny us; if we are faithless, he remains faithful—for he cannot deny himself."

The first three propositions are logical if-then statements of the sort that are the lynchpin of computer programming. If such a condition is fulfilled, then this or that will happen. If we are faithful, God will reward us. If we deny God, God will deny us. But the last one is illogical—and loving. "If we are faithless, he remains faithful—for he cannot deny himself." This is the warp and woof of all of scripture—God's faithful love for the people, mirrored by us at the best of times (such as in the Book of Ruth); and when we fail to mirror that love, then God's love is even more persistent, even to the cross.

This is the unchanging God who changes because of love for us. If we proof-text God, taking out individual verses and insisting they tell the whole story, we could be dashed against the rocks. But there's grace, bending with the breeze, preserving us whole.

How do we mirror that love in our relationships? In our own lives, do you want to proof-text a person and base everything you know about that person on a series of isolated moments, or is it more important to consider the whole of a relationship?

In our dealings with each other, we sometimes founder on the rules. The rules are the rules. They don't change. Play by the rules or go elsewhere. Jesus warned us that the sabbath was made for the benefit of humanity, not humanity for the sabbath, yet even in our own churches we can get so bogged down by our motions and seconds, our written and unwritten rules, that there is no room for grace, no place for change.

There's a balance in scripture between a changing and unchanging God. I don't have to explain how it works, don't have to justify it, and I can't predict when it will happen. But with this God, a person like me stands half a chance.

Change is a constant in our lives. As children we prefer to believe that our parents are perfect and do not change, but they do. As employees we want our jobs to never change and remain in one place. This has not been the experience of most people. As partners in marriage and friendship, we want unchanging lovers and friends. As citizens we want the world to stand still once in a while. Our experience is that paradigms not only change but are thrown into the trash can and new rules have to be established. What then can we count on? What is more comforting, a God who never changes or a God who bargains when confronted with our frailty? Are the two views mutually exclusive?

Finally, as a people we are presented with the unchanging word of God. This is a tremendous gift. But our understandings and our interpretations of scripture change. As a people who are in charge, how do we deal with the text and its meaning? Are we willing to change? Does mercy and love govern our interpretation? How much do we trust ourselves, as a study group, to wrestle with God's word, circumstance, and the gift of grace that live among us, and come to see things in a new light?

Discussion and Action

1. How have you changed over the years? In what ways are you the same? In the time your present group has been meeting, what kinds of change have you experienced as a group? How has that affected the way you study the Bible together?

2. Here are some background scriptures that speak to the issue of an unchanging and a changing God: Numbers 23:19; 1 Samuel 15:29; Romans 11:29; James 1:17; Lamentations 3:22; 2 Samuel 24:16; Jeremiah 26:19; 1 Kings 3:6; 2 Chronicles 32:24; Isaiah 38:1-6. This is not a complete list. Take time to read these verses aloud. If time allows, look at the context for the verses or consult a commentary to get a broader perspective on how these verses speak to this issue. What other scriptures might you add to this list?

3. Do you think there is a contradiction between a changing and an unchanging God? If so, how do you interpret the apparent differences in these passages? If not, how do you interpret these apparent differences?

4. God's word does not change. But is it possible to gain a new understanding of an old text? If so, how can God's people go about this?

5. If you took time to work out a new tune or new words for a favorite hymn, consider sharing that with others in the group by singing the "new" hymn or by speaking the words.

6. What face does your church or group show to the community or world? What are the positive aspects of your identity? What are the negative aspects? Consider ways (through landscaping, press releases, programs, and building face-lifts, focusing your ministry, etc.) that you might present a new face to others.

6

Four Gospels, One Lord
Mark 9:38-41 and Matthew 12:22-32

Personal Preparation

1. Think back to those occasions when you first heard the Gospels read aloud. Was it from the pulpit, at home, in a small group? What passages do you remember hearing? What were your impressions? What did you visualize? What hit home?

2. Make a list of your various relationships. What titles do you have in those relationships, groups, jobs, or ministries? How do people know you? Bring the list to the session.

3. Read John 20:30-31 and John 21:25. Why do you suppose there are four Gospels instead of one—or one hundred?

4. Read Mark 9:38-41 and Matthew 12:22-32 aloud to yourself. Write out Mark 9:40 and Matthew 12:30. Do you think these verses say the same thing or different things? If they say different things, what do they say?

Suggestions for Sharing and Prayer

1. Greet one another, sharing events of the past week. Respond to any joys or concerns with one-sentence prayers. Close with prayer for God's guidance in your study today.

2. Arrange yourselves in a circle. Write a one-minute biography for the person to your right and for the person to your left. At the end of two minutes, after everyone has

done this, share these biographies with one another. There should be two bios written about each person. Point out differences, discrepancies, and similarities between the two stories.

3. Share the lists of your relationships (from Personal Preparation 2). Thinking specifically about the groups and societies to which you belong, discuss some of the following questions. Which have closed membership? Which have membership that is constantly changing? Are newcomers welcome in these groups to which you belong? How do you think these groups are perceived by people outside the groups? How are these groups viewed from within?

4. The Gospel of Mark was the first to be written down. React to these statements by Reynolds Price, who said Mark "has proved the most influential of all human books." He writes, "The audacious claims it makes for the single life and the career it describes have pressed more heavily on two millennia of geopolitical history, for good and ill, than even the lunatic call to action of Hitler . . . or the immense and passionate bellow for justice in the lifework of Karl Marx."

5. Talk together about why you think there are four Gospels instead of one? Would that have been simpler? better?

6. As in Personal Preparation 4, read Mark 9:38-41 and Matthew 12:22-32 aloud. Do you think Mark 9:40 and Matthew 12:30 say the same thing or different things? If they say different things, what do they say?

7. Pray Psalm 23 aloud together. After each clause, pause for silent reflection, inviting sentence prayers that expand or comment upon that clause.

8. Sing "What a friend we have in Jesus."

Understanding

In Samuel Beckett's classic play *Waiting for Godot,* two tramps wait for Godot. They talk to pass the time.

One of the tramps recalls the story of the two thieves who hung on crosses next to Jesus: "How is it that of the four Evangelists, only one speaks of a thief being saved?" After more reflection he adds, "One out of four. Of the other three, two don't mention any thieves at all and the third says that both of them abused him."

The other tramp grows impatient with the discussion and finally concludes, "They don't agree and that's all there is to it."

It's one thing to discuss apparent contradictions in the Bible when it's the Old Testament, but it's another thing when it involves Jesus. We don't like it. It's not comfortable. But the other tramp is right. Sometimes the Gospels don't agree, and that's all there is to it. And in those cases what are we to do?

Are We Talking About the Same Guy?
Why four Gospels in the first place? Why not one authoritative life of Jesus, and be done with it?

My friend Junelle Miller once asked three siblings to join her in writing down recollections of their father for the benefit of their youngest brother who really did not remember him. When Junelle looked over the four biographies she had to wonder if they were writing about the same person. The accounts were true, but they were very different because of their different perspectives and the different ways in which their father had opened up his life to each of them.

When it comes to the Gospel accounts of the life of Jesus, we, as well, might sometimes wonder if we're dealing with the same person! Matthew, Mark, and Luke seem to be recounting the same incidents, but each approaches the material in a different way. As for the evangelist John—his account differs radically from the others.

Vernard Eller asked us to imagine that the Gospels are four separate puzzles. Some people are tempted to dump all four puzzles onto the same table and make a single puzzle of them, jamming in pieces whether they fit or not. He advocated that we take each Gospel as a separate viewpoint and learn what we can from it.

No one wrote a Gospel right after the death and resurrection of Jesus. Those who heard Jesus speak repeated his words, and they in turn shared them with others. For a time, people had a reliable living link to the actual events. But over time the original witnesses began to die, and the gospel spread farther away. The biblical writers drew upon the words and actions of Jesus, but tailored their accounts to the needs of the people who received them so that their questions could be answered and their lives strengthened.

Rather than go through a detailed analysis of the ways the Gospels are interrelated and independent of each other, we will examine only one saying that appears in both Mark and Matthew—in two versions that seem to directly contradict each other.

For Mark, the cross is the intersection between God and humanity, and it is not possible to know Jesus without the cross. His purpose may have been to demonstrate that the kingdom of God was inaugurated by the life and work of Jesus.

Matthew's Gospel demonstrates that the life of Jesus occurred in fulfillment of the Hebrew scriptures. What happened was ordained by God and came to pass as it ought.

Luke was a companion of Paul and also the author of the Acts of the Apostles. He wrote to a Roman world that set great store in rhetoric, the art of speaking to convince. Unlike today, where talking heads put great reliance on spin and loudly talking over one another, rhetoric assumes that individuals on both sides of the discussion will listen with open minds.

Then there's John. There was a time when John was dismissed as a mystic whose Gospel was not grounded in literal truth. But archaeology has demonstrated that John is a reliable witness.

Pay Attention

In Mark 9:40, Jesus says, "Whoever is not against us is for us." In Matthew 12:30, Jesus says, "Whoever is not with me is against me." These are two very different statements. Did Jesus say one or the other, or both?

One of the mistakes people make in biblical interpretation is what is called "proof texting," which means taking a verse out of context in order to back up an argument. But remember, the original manuscripts of the Bible were not divided into verses and chapters (for the New Testament, that didn't happen until 1551). The oldest biblical manuscripts were usually written with no punctuation or even spaces between words, which means that it is usually better to work with blocks of biblical text, rather than isolated verses.

Mark's version follows a larger discussion about which disciple is the greatest (9:33-37). Jesus says, "Whoever wants to be first must be last of all and servant of all" (Mark 9:35). He then takes up a child in his arms. Children were not valued as they are today—they gained value as they grew able to work. But Jesus takes this marginalized member of society and says, "Whoever welcomes one such child in my name welcomes me, and whoever welcomes me welcomes not me but the one who sent me" (9:37).

Having described a situation in which servanthood and acceptance of the marginalized are the true hallmarks of a disciple, can there be any wonder that in the context of this story Jesus would expect his disciples to abandon jealousy and rivalry for inclusion and acceptance?

When the disciples tell Jesus they have stopped an outsider from healing others in his name, Jesus responds, "Whoever is not against us is for us. For truly I tell you, whoever gives you a cup of water to drink because you bear the name of Christ will by no means lose the reward" (9:40-41).

On the other hand, Matthew has Jesus being challenged in several successive stories by religious authorities who accuse him and his followers of acting against the faith, and they finally go so far as to claim that the work of Jesus is demonic.

In this context Jesus says, "Whoever is not with me is against me, and whoever does not gather with me scatters. Therefore I tell you, people will be forgiven for every sin and blasphemy, but blasphemy against the Spirit will not be forgiven" (Matt. 12:30-31). By the way, the story appears pretty much the same way in Luke as in Matthew.

Jesus could have said both of these things. On the one hand, as Christians it is important that we accept others who are doing the work of Jesus and be prepared to accept a cup of cold water from them rather than rejecting them for not measuring up to our standards, especially when they threaten our own imagined place in the gospel kingdom. On the other hand, Matthew's version warns us that those who demonize their opponents, who demean and dismiss others, are in danger of blaspheming against the Spirit present in all of us.

The Bible is not a convenient tool to use to back up our own established notions, but it is a guide and a gift from God to walk with us in our own discovery. A healthier, more authentic and biblical approach might be to understand each Gospel's viewpoint and goal, and how it fits within the larger Christian proclamation. Mature adults realize that honest people can be present at the same events and yet view them in radically different ways.

Instead of trying to fit all four Gospels into one large jigsaw puzzle, it is better to treat each Gospel separately, as separate puzzles that we put together in a small group study so that we can experience and live these words together. Though we may find, as did the tramp in *Waiting for Godot,* that the four don't agree and that's all there is to it, we probably won't worry too much because we'll be too busy strengthening our relationship with God, God's word, and each other.

Discussion and Action

1. As individuals, write down definitions of the words *Christian* and *Christianity.* Share your definitions with one another. What are the similarities in your definitions? What differences emerge? Could each definition be true in a specific context?

2. The two Gospel texts for this session center around the definition of "the group." Are we inclusive or exclusive? Is it possible for those on the inside to know if they are inclusive or exclusive, or can that only be defined from the outside? Explain your answers.

3. When is the first saying (Mark 9:40) useful? When is the second saying (Matt. 12:30) useful? Under what circumstances might they not be useful? It might be instructive

to divide into two groups and prepare to discuss these passages using the rhetorical style. After the "Mark" team defends its position, the "Matthew" team presents its case. Following the arguments, reflect together on the strengths and weaknesses of each position.

4. Mark's version of the saying suggests that anyone, regardless of background, is to be considered a follower of Jesus if that person is not actively working against the gospel. That is a very inclusive statement indeed, but it is not original with Jesus. The saying itself is quoted by Cicero, who lived in the first century B.C. The conclusion is that the good works of those who give a cup of cold water will not lose their reward. Does this sound true to you? Why? What does Matthew's version seem to say in response?

5. Which of the two Gospel passages for today's session moves you more and represents your viewpoint? Why?

6. In which ways do we work well together as Christians? In what ways do we fail to work together as Christians? End with prayer that we might continue to grow and mature in our relationships with one another.

7

The Birth of Jesus
Matthew 1–2 and Luke 1–2

Personal Preparation

1. Regardless of the season, play some Christmas music while you go about your regular business. Write down your five favorite Christmas carols or hymns. What do they have in common? Why do you like them?
2. Pick a day and read the Christmas passages from Matthew. Add up the generations listed in chapter 1. Draw a picture to illustrate the story.
3. The genealogy that appears in Matthew includes several women who have interesting stories. Write down their names, and then look them up in a Bible dictionary. Using a concordance, find and read their stories in the Bible.
4. On a different day, read the Christmas passages from Luke. Draw another picture to illustrate this story.
5. Pray Psalm 111 aloud.

Suggestions for Sharing and Prayer

The first two chapters of Luke contain several famous prayers that have become part of Christian tradition. These are known as the Magnificat, the Benedictus, and the Nunc Dimitus. Along with the words of the angel Gabriel, these three prayers will comprise the prayer time for this session.

1. Greet one another as you arrive and share some of the events of this past week. Share sentence prayers in response to each joy or concern.

2. Role-play the conversation Mary has with her parents and with Joseph, telling them what the angel Gabriel has told her.

3. In the Magnificat (Luke 1:46-55), Mary connects God's blessings for her life to God's history with the people in the past and with God's intentions for the future. Review the words of this prayer and try to imagine what this prayer might mean for people who are poor, who are outcast, who are rich, who are powerful. Pray the Magnificat aloud together.

4. Zechariah had been rendered unable to speak because he questioned the angel who told him of the upcoming birth of his son. In the Benedictus (Luke 1:67-79), his tongue is loosed and he sings praises for what God will do through his son and for all people. Review the words of this prayer and consider what the words might mean for you. Pray the Benedictus aloud together.

5. Read aloud the Angels' song (Luke 2:14). How do you suppose the shepherds understood this song? What should our response be to this message? Proclaim the message to one another.

6. The Nunc Dimitus (Luke 2:29-32) is Simeon's prayer after the Spirit informs him that the Messiah has come to the temple and he then meets the infant Jesus. Have you achieved the sort of peace with life that Simeon expresses? What sort of trust do you have in God? What is missing from your life, if anything, that could help you achieve the peace expressed in this statement? Pray the Nunc Dimitus aloud together.

7. Close by singing the carol "What child is this?"

Understanding

Have you ever taken one of those Christmas quizzes with questions like how many kings came to see Jesus (none, they were magi and the Bible doesn't tell us the number), how many angels sang to the shepherds (the Bible doesn't tell us the number), and what day was Jesus born (nobody knows!)?

Most people get the answers wrong because they base their Christmas knowledge on TV specials, greeting cards, and carols—not on the Bible. Not only that, they mix up two very different narratives, so that kings stand next to shepherds even though there is every reason to think the magi did not arrive until Jesus was over a year old!

Birth narratives in the ancient world emphasized the importance of the person who was born, which is why both Matthew and Luke make it clear that despite the trappings of royal power in the emperor's palace and Herod's halls, the real king is this child born to a displaced Palestinian family!

The account in Matthew is told from Joseph's point of view. Matthew's genealogy traces Joseph's line, even though Jesus is not his biological son. It's as if he is saying, "It's not who has the baby, but who loves the baby, that matters."

Mary, who here is simply "found to be with child from the Holy Spirit," is wrongly accused of adultery. Joseph must make a choice. In the eyes of the law, betrothal was the same as being married. Joseph would have been within his rights to insist upon her execution. Instead, Joseph, who is described as "a righteous man and unwilling to expose [Mary] to public disgrace," makes arrangements to divorce her quietly.

Joseph chooses to do not only what is right, but what is good. As Jesus himself will say later in the Gospel of Matthew, "For with the judgment you make you will be judged, and the measure you give will be the measure you get" (7:2). Joseph grants mercy and mercifully does not unjustly kill another.

The appearance of an angel in a dream sets Joseph straight. Consistent with Matthew's theme, it is made clear that the birth of Jesus will be in accordance with the Hebrew scriptures. The first chapter ends with the pronouncement that normal sexual relations between Joseph and Mary did not begin until after the birth of Jesus.

The story continues with triumph and tragedy. The magi recognize signs pointing to the birth of Jesus, even while God's people miss those signs totally. The star they saw was probably a conjunction of Jupiter with Venus, near Regulus, the king star, which is part of the constellation Leo and which was associated in the ancient world with the Lion of Judah and God's people. This odd formation occurred twice during the years 3 and 2 B.C., and means that the magi, who were stargazers and astrologers, probably interpreted this sign to mean that a king had been born in Judea. Herod the Great and the Jewish court paid no attention to the stars and missed the sign entirely.

The magi bear gifts recognizing Jesus as the one who will bring about God's kingdom of justice. This is in fulfillment of scriptures, such as Psalm 72:10-11; Isaiah 2:1-4 and 60:4-11; and Micah 4:1-4, which point to a time when Gentiles will bring their gifts to God's permanent kingdom of justice.

Alas, the magi unintentionally set into motion a tragic chain of events, as Herod the Great, a jealous and irrational ruler, decided to kill children two years old and younger in an attempt to extinguish what he saw as a threat to his throne. Jesus and his family become refugees and cannot return until Herod is dead. Herod's death around 1 B.C., is tied by ancient historians to a lunar eclipse, which occurred that year near Passover.

Matthew's point is that the birth of Jesus happens according to the Hebrew scriptures, and that outsiders will be the ones who recognize the blessing and strive to be a part of it, while insiders miss the blessing entirely.

Luke tells the story from the viewpoint of the women, Elizabeth and Mary, and also from that of the Old Testament prophet Isaiah. In Luke 4:18, Jesus preaches from Isaiah 61:1-2a, "The Spirit of the Lord is upon me, because he has anointed me to bring good news to the poor. He has sent me to proclaim release to the captives and recovery of sight to the blind, to let the oppressed go free, to proclaim the year of the Lord's favor." Luke intends to show that this is the program of Jesus and his followers.

Both Elizabeth and Mary recognize that the Lord has taken their side because the Lord takes the side of the oppressed and marginalized. Elizabeth's pronouncements in Luke 1:25 and 1:42-45, as well as Mary's song of praise in 1:47-56, celebrate the way God's story has been made visible in their lives. Both women draw upon Old Testament scriptures so that their new songs are also old and familiar songs. Zechariah, upon the birth of John the Baptist (1:67-79), and Simeon, who recognizes Jesus as the Messiah (2:29-32), echo this theme.

Jesus' birth narrative takes place against a canvas as large as the Roman Empire, as an emperor, who claimed to be a god, commands a worldwide tax registration. The irony is that the real God-King is born in humble circumstances and that shepherds, who in Jesus' day were considered untrustworthy and lived on the margins of society, are the ones to whom the angels tell the glorious news; they, in turn are the first ones to proclaim the gospel.

When Zechariah talks of a God he calls "Most High" (1:76), he uses the term used by Gentiles for the God of the Hebrews, thus accentuating Luke's point that this good news is for all people, especially those previously on the margins of God's plan.

One misconception is that Jesus was born in a barn. Actually Palestinian homes tended to have a single floor with two levels. Animals were essential to a family's economy and needed to be well treated. The people lived on the level that was slightly higher; animals lived on the lower level. What this suggests is that when Mary and Joseph could find no room at an inn in Bethlehem, they stayed at someone's house, possibly someone else with roots in Galilee. There might well have been several families together under that roof, and when Mary started to give birth, the event, far from happening in isolation in a building out back, was shared by many people who helped, yelped, or otherwise took part.

I grew up with the pageant known as "Las Posadas," in which Mary and Joseph go from place to place and are refused entry. It's ingrained in me that no room at the inn meant *no room,* but this different picture reminds us that people likely did make room for the family without shelter, which puts more pressure on us than ever to take care of refugees and those who have nowhere to go.

The birth accounts in Matthew and Luke challenge us to examine the Bible ourselves, and not trust what we already "know" simply because that is conventional wisdom. When it comes to controversial topics, many Christians feel they already know what the Bible says, but they may have never examined the texts for themselves. Do not entrust to pundits what the Bible might say about a particular subject, especially controversial topics. Go look for yourselves. Use commentaries and other Bible helps to go beyond what seems to be the obvious meaning. We are God's people, and we are called to interpret God's word—together!

Discussion and Action

1. Read again the Angels' Song in Luke 2:14. Pray that God will show you how your group might share this good news with the community and the world. If something concrete arises in your discernment, make a plan for turning the inspiration into action.

2. The genealogy in Matthew states there are three different sets of fourteen generations in the lineage of Jesus, yet one of the sets names only thirteen generations. What do we make of such a deficiency? How do you think it came about? Does it matter? If someone in your group is so inclined, commission them to do some research on what biblical scholars have to say about this.

3. As a group, design a Christmas card that tells the nativity story as found in Matthew. Then, design together another Christmas card that tells the nativity story as found in Luke. What similarities and differences do you see? What difference do these distinctives make? Do you think people who receive either card would notice the difference? Why or why not?

4. There is a saying that "God doesn't have any grandchildren," meaning that we are all adopted, first-generation children of God. The women who are part of the genealogy of Jesus in Matthew are outsiders, as are the magi. The shepherds in Luke's Gospel are outcasts. What does this say about God's family and our place in it?

5. Share the favorite Christmas songs you listed in Personal Preparation 1. Discuss the common and unique elements of your lists. Sing a few of the carols together, perhaps picking several with common elements, then several others with contrasting elements.

8

The Most Famous Sermon
Matthew 4:24–5:12, 38-42 and Luke 6:17-23
Luke 11:2-4 and Matthew 6:9-13
Matthew 7:12 and Luke 6:31

Personal Preparation

1. On a piece of paper, write out Matthew 5:3-12 in one column, leaving some space between the verses. Then write out Luke 6:17-23. When it is possible, write a verse from Luke across from one that seems to match it in Matthew. Write the other verses from Luke across from blank space in the Matthew column. Read both columns aloud. Bring your paper to the session.
2. Consider which of "the blessed" in both lists might apply to you. Then read Luke 6:24-26, and consider which of Luke's woes might apply to you.
3. Read the Lord's Prayer in both Matthew 6:9-13 and Luke 11:2-4. Take a moment to pray both versions aloud, reflecting on the meaning of each phrase.

Suggestions for Sharing and Prayer

1. Begin with greetings, and then share from the past week. When the group seems ready, gather together for sentence prayers.
2. As a group, select a hymn to sing together at the close of the prayer time.
3. Recite Psalm 119:1-8 in unison.

4. Pray the Lord's Prayer, pausing after each phrase. Go around the group, uttering the first thought that comes to mind. For instance, after "Our Father," someone might suggest another way to address God; another person might simply repeat, "Our Father." Or, the phrase "Give us this day our daily bread" might elicit other petitions for yourselves, for loved ones, or for others.

5. Read aloud Matthew 7:12, popularly known as the Golden Rule. On newsprint, write two column headings: Do GOOD and Do NO HARM. Drawing upon personal experiences and news stories of the past week, invite reflection on some recent situations for which the Golden Rule might provide guidance. Consider what might be proper response to these situations, based either on *doing good* or on *doing no harm*. What difference is there between these two approaches? How do the scriptures indicate which might be the best approach to take?

6. Invite each person to write his or her name on a strip of paper, and drop it into a hat or jar. Then invite each member to pick a name (be sure not to get your own). Take a few moments to compose a spoken or silent blessing for the person whose name was drawn. Share these in turn. If you pray your blessing silently, conclude by saying "Amen" aloud.

7. Close by reading Revelation 22:14 aloud. Sing the hymn you selected earlier and then pray Luke 11:2-4 together.

Understanding

Back in 1920, a quiet scholar named Edgar J. Goodspeed found himself at the center of a firestorm when a news service got hold of a page proof of his New Testament translation and concluded that he had shortened the Lord's Prayer! Criticism was intense and vicious as commentators assumed he was dumbing down the New Testament for a modern age. One newspaper thundered that "a gentleman of such limitations would jazz a Beethoven sonata."

Of course, these people were showing their own ignorance. The Lord's Prayer appears in a different form in Luke than it does in Matthew. The same goes for much of what is called the Sermon on the Mount.

Let us examine three famous portions of the Sermon on the Mount—the Beatitudes, the Golden Rule, and the Lord's Prayer—and compare the way they are treated in the two Gospels.

The Beatitudes

The Beatitudes are more than just a series of fond wishes or good feelings. The sentiments are not conditional; they are fact. We don't just wish it were so that the meek should inherit the earth, or hope that it might prove true in some mystical way. These statements are backed up by God.

In both Matthew's Sermon on the Mount and Luke's Sermon on the Plain, the first beatitude sets the tone for the whole series. Matthew was writing to a Jewish Christian audience, familiar with what they called the Two Ways: there is good and bad, and people choose between the two. So Matthew divides the world between the righteous and the unrighteous. The "poor in spirit" are the righteous ones who live like Jesus.

Luke was writing to Jews and Gentiles in the Roman Empire. He—and they—divided the world into rich and poor. Jesus turned the world upside down by restating what is clear throughout the scriptures—unlike the world, God takes the side of the poor!

Matthew wrote that the life of Jesus was the fulfillment of the Hebrew scriptures; Luke's audience may not have read them. Citizens of the empire might not care about Hebrew scriptures, but they were ready to follow Jesus because of his advocacy for the poor and outcasts.

Both outlooks are helpful. Luke helps us avoid the mistake of spiritualizing the Beatitudes when he begins by stating, "Blessed are the poor." He is talking about actual poor people. But Matthew's approach helps us avoid the mistake of assuming that simply by being poor one is also saved. After all, there are plenty of people, both poor and rich, who are scoundrels, pure and simple.

Both versions call us to radically change our view of the world. Jesus makes it clear that the call to discipleship is difficult (why else are we warned in these passages that we will suffer for the sake of righteousness?), but that it has heavenly rewards.

The flipside to the Beatitudes are the Woes. Since Jesus addresses these words to his disciples, we must assume that some of them were rich. Both rich and poor were part of the community of Jesus and needed to strive to be poor in spirit—and to be advocates for the poor.

The promise of the Beatitudes helps prepare believers for an even more radical step—responding to the call to love our enemies. The call to love our enemies is not a naive sentiment, but an essential element of following Jesus. It makes no sense, unless we are truly ready to take up our cross and follow the one who has told us that we are blessed and will inherit the earth.

The Golden Rule

The Golden Rule predates the Gospels. It appears in many different cultures, either in the positive form familiar to us (Do unto others as you would have them do unto you) or in its negative form (Do not do unto others as you would not want them to do unto you). Certainly it was present in Jewish thought at the time of Jesus.

There is no guarantee associated with this saying. A person might do good, or at least avoid harming others, and still be the brunt of evildoers.

Some would say that the negative form of the saying invites a safe "Do no harm" sort of attitude, while the positive version in Matthew and Luke invites risk. Luke, writing to the larger world, knows that many of his readers will know nothing of the law and the prophets, but would know that the Golden Rule was a principle for life accepted by people throughout the Roman Empire. It was self-evident and needed no proof.

Both approaches are necessary in the current age. Many Christians find themselves in Matthew's world, where the Golden Rule is part of a larger understanding of the Bible's way of life. But many people in our society, including many who are coming back to church, are not familiar with the scriptures in general or the words of Jesus in particular. Moreover, simply saying that something is proved by scripture isn't good enough for those who have taken part in the larger society. They need to see that the truth of scripture is confirmed by the world they observe.

The Lord's Prayer

The Lord's Prayer is disarming in its brevity and simplicity, yet there is depth to the prayer. It can be divided into three parts. The first is an invocation, with praise for God and a call for God's will to be done. Then there is a central petition for daily bread, which has been interpreted both literally and symbolically. People need bread to eat, and they need a lot more than bread to truly live. Finally, there is a request for forgiveness paired with the requirement that we emulate God in forgiving, along with a petition calling for God's protection against the occasions of sin.

Jesus' prayer draws heavily from prayers present in Jewish thought of the time. Its originality is apparent in Jesus' choice and organization of thought. Beginning with the opening phrase, "Our Father," which suggests that God is God of all people, the prayer draws us into a serious, personal, and trusting relationship with the divine.

While some have tried to settle which version is the original, others suggest a better question to ask is how Jesus used the same prayer for different purposes. Matthew's version would better suit a group brought up in the faith, familiar with the cadences of church language, and who might benefit from ordering their thoughts according to God's design. Luke's shorter prayer draws those who are not churched (such as his original Gentile audience and people of our own time) away from a prejudice against complexity toward simplicity in expression and purpose.

We can no longer assume that the world around us either needs or is interested in church for its own sake. Many in the larger society see church as irrelevant and unnecessary. Yet studies also show that the vast majority of people believe in a personal and active God. Why don't those same people come to church? Maybe a better question is why hasn't the church gone to them?

The Sermon on the Mount presents a radically different way to live. If there is a post-modern or post-Christian world out there, then it is very similar to the world in which Jesus and his disciples found themselves. Taking the side of the poor as God has, doing for others as we would have them do for us, and sharing a personal, even intimate, relationship with God and with other disciples may be the best way to reach out to this world.

Discussion and Action

1. What are your earliest memories of the Lord's Prayer? Do you feel you have understood its meaning from the beginning, or has your understanding and appreciation for the prayer changed over time? Explain. When you recall the Lord's Prayer, do you have a strong sense one way or the other that you're simply reciting words or that you're offering a heartfelt prayer? Why?

2. Share instances when the Lord's Prayer has held the most meaning for you. Conversely, share times when it hasn't been so meaningful. What has made the difference?

3. Talk together about who you might consider to be an enemy. Depending on the mix of people in your group, it may help stimulate conversation by setting a ground rule of speaking in general terms rather than naming specific people. How easy (or difficult) is it to come up with a list of those you consider to be enemies? At issue may be whether or not you believe you have enemies. Whether your enemies list includes specific people or more general categories of people, how difficult is it to love these people?

4. Jesus invites us to do for others as we would have them do for us. What person or group in your church or community needs the blessings the Sermon on the Mount seems to invite? Is it possible to do for these others? If so, how might you respond?

5. Write your own "Lord's Prayer," listing those petitions that are important to the group.

6. Close by praying your version of the Lord's Prayer, along with whichever biblical version you are most familiar.

9

Which Day Was It?
John 13:1-20 and Mark 14:12-14

Personal Preparation

1. Read the passages for this week aloud.
2. Write your impressions of these two passages on a piece of paper or in a journal. Consider the following question: "Are these two evangelists writing about the same thing?"
3. Think about important events in your life. Can you remember the dates on which they took place? Do you remember which days of the week they occurred? What helps you to keep these things in your memory?
4. Pray Psalm 41 aloud. Reflect on those who have mistreated you and on those whom you may have mistreated, intentionally or unintentionally.

Suggestions for Sharing and Prayer

1. Greet each other as you arrive and take time to share news from the past week. Offer sentence prayers in response to what is shared.
2. Read Psalm 41 aloud, taking turns reading a verse at a time.
3. Call upon one person to lead the group in extended prayer.
4. Name some of the holidays and holy days you commemorate. Consider together the origin of these days as you understand them (you may want to consult the Internet or an encyclopedia), as well as the day or date on which they fall this year.

5. Think of celebrations that take place on different days in different places or traditions, such as Thanksgiving in the U.S. and Canada, Christmas practices in North America and other parts of the world, or Easter in various Christian communions. Why do you think this is so?

6. Reflect upon your understandings of the Last Supper and the communion practices of which you've been a part. What differences and similarities do you note? What are the origins, in your opinion, for these practices? Why do variations of some of these practices exist? In your opinion, is some variety okay, or should Christians aim for uniformity in practice?

7. Read the two passages for this session aloud.

8. Think back on important occasions in the life of your group and in the life of your congregation. What were these events? When did they take place? How do you mark that day in your memory? In what ways were those days observed? What is their significance now? Is that significance the same as when the day itself occurred, or has its meaning changed over time? If so, how?

9. Sing "Were you there?"

Understanding

Someone once introduced me by telling a story from seminary days. According to the story, I convinced some fellow students to skip class to watch the Cubs play baseball. The secret was out when we were interviewed on the local television station, where I mentioned that God was a big baseball fan because the Bible says God created the world "in the big inning." All the faculty saw the broadcast, and to make matters worse, we were featured on the front page of the *Chicago Tribune* the next day.

It's a great story, and it's all true—even if none of the facts are right! In reality, we went to see the White Sox, not the Cubs. We were interviewed on two radio stations, not on television. There was no appearance in print. The faculty didn't see us; it was the head librarian at Northern Baptist, our sister seminary.

And although I did mention the "big inning" line, I had a whole shtick prepared and that was just one of the jokes.

Baseball is one thing and the Bible is another. Sometimes two separate accounts of the same event cannot be reconciled, yet they're both true. Both Mark and John are based on eyewitness accounts—Mark's on the memories of Peter, and John's on those of the beloved disciple. In their stories of the Last Supper, they conflict on one key point. Both Gospels place the meal on Thursday, but in Mark's Gospel the Last Supper takes place on the first day of Passover (Mark 14:12). In John's Gospel it takes place on the day of preparation—before Passover begins (John 13:1).

Which was it?

Jews of the first century were split into many denominations, like Christianity is today. And like today, they may have celebrated major religious festivals on different days. Some suggest that Jews who lived in Palestine celebrated Passover on the sabbath day, Saturday, while Jews who lived in the empire ate the meal on Friday.

It's no different for Christians, some of whom celebrate the birth of Jesus on December 25, while others make it a longer festival that peaks on January 6. Some in Europe exchange their Christmas gifts on December 6, St. Nicholas Day. And when it comes to Easter, some Orthodox groups use an older calendar that places Easter days or even weeks after the Western churches.

Calendars may be at the heart of the reason that Mark and John seem to pick different days for the Last Supper. There is reason to believe that Jews from Jerusalem, Judea, Galilee, as well as the ascetic Dead Sea Scroll group known as the Essenes, marked Passover on different days. In part that might have been because some kept a 354-day lunar calendar (built around the phases of the moon), while others observed a 365-day solar calendar.

If they are both reliable, why would two witnesses select a totally different day for this most crucial event? One of the important things to look at is the intent of the Gospel writers. Why would the Gospel writers put the meal in different parts of the holy days? What point were they trying to make?

Mark's Gospel makes the Last Supper the Passover meal. This is clearly demonstrated by the fact that Jesus came back to Jerusalem for the meal instead of going back to nearby Bethany for safety as he did on other nights. The Passover meal was supposed to be eaten inside Jerusalem. Other clues are the fact that the meal took place in the evening, that bread was broken, wine was served, and a hymn was sung at the end of the meal. In this tradition (shared by Matthew and Luke), the Last Supper is the crucial foundation for the communion service. It takes place on the first evening of Passover. Communion is the new Passover.

John, who already put communion language in the sixth chapter of his Gospel, just as clearly identifies this gathering as having taken place before the slaughter of the lambs, that is, before the first day of Passover, which would not begin until nightfall of the following day. On this evening before Passover begins, feetwashing is the critical thing, not the meal. Washing feet makes Jesus' love for his own visible and concrete. The fellowship meal that follows creates the new body of Christ.

One reason for the different choices made by the two writers may have been the lambs that were eaten on Passover. They were killed on the first day of the observance. That means in Mark's Gospel that Jesus is eating lamb with his disciples as he establishes the bread and cup communion. Communion becomes the new Passover. Instead of deliverance from slavery to Pharaoh and the beginning of the journey to the Promised Land, Christians would celebrate the deliverance from slavery to the world and the beginning of the journey that transformed them into a people on the way to the New Jerusalem.

In John, Jesus is the Lamb of God. That is evident in the language he uses. Jesus dies and becomes the perfect sacrifice. And the meal established prior to this event was not communion, but a fellowship meal.

Can we incorporate both viewpoints into a single service? If so, what would that service look like? Perhaps it would look a lot like the love feast celebrated by some denominations, a service that includes feetwashing either for all in attendance or for select representatives, as well as a full meal, followed by the bread and cup.

Which one really happened? Is it possible here to say both/and, rather than either/or?

One of the problems is that you can't get there from here. Two thousand years later and we're really not sure what year Jesus was born, nor what year he was crucified. If we could answer those questions, we could solve the problem with a planetarium show, pinpointing when the proper spring new moon arrived, allowing us to figure out which Thursday and Friday served as the Last Supper and crucifixion, and therefore which meal, the Passover or the Preparation, was shared by the apostles.

If I had to choose, I would pick John over Mark. The Jewish day began with sundown. If Mark, Matthew, and Luke are right, and the Thursday night of the Last Supper was the start of Passover, then the Friday that followed was also the first day of Passover until sundown. Mark wants us to believe that it was possible for a crucifixion to take place on the Passover. Some commentators suggest that given what we know about first-century society, that's impossible.

Rather than settle the matter, I'd prefer to incorporate both understandings—the servanthood of Jesus and we disciples who follow, embodied in the sacrifice of the Lamb of God, and the remembrance of the death of Jesus, which is the meaning of Mark's Gospel.

How does this affect us? Probably not much when it comes to Maundy Thursday, Good Friday, and Easter Sunday. Our habits are ingrained. But when it comes to our lives together, the significance of shared events varies with the participants. Just as Mark and John look at the same events very differently and our perception is richer because we tend to take both into account, so it is not possible to fully understand an event without taking into account everyone's perceptions.

The passion of Jesus is the foundation of much of western civilization, Christian and non-Christian alike. If we put ourselves into the event, answering the question of the hymn "Were you there?" where exactly will we find ourselves, and where will others be? Can we see the events of our lives together as a faith community through many eyes, or must we focus on making sure that our version of events is the only acceptable one?

Discussion and Action

1. Think of situations when you and someone else may have shared an experience but described it totally differently. Why do you think there is sometimes a difference in the way people look at things? Reflect on your conversation earlier (Suggestions for Sharing and Prayer 8) about important events in your life together. Did you all recall these events in the same ways? Were all the details or even the impacts of these events the same, or is there some variation in your memories? If so, what accounts for these differences? How does it make you feel to know that someone else may not realize what's important to you, and that you may not recall what's significant to someone else? Is there value in harmonizing your memories? Explain.

2. Has studying this session changed anything about how you look at the Last Supper or at communion? If so, what? If not, why not? What do these events in the life of the church mean to you as individuals and as a group?

3. Must we all look at holidays and holy days in the same way? What are the blessings and the dangers if individuals within the fellowship choose to observe holy days in different ways and at different times? What level of agreement must we have in order to be unified?

4. Wonder aloud about the way the apostles might have felt during the Last Supper as described by Mark. What impact or significance might this event have had on them?

5. Wonder aloud about the way the apostles might have felt during the Last Supper as described by John. What impact or significance might this event have had on them?

6. What constitutes a true story? Can there be more than one version of the truth?

7. When a small group studies together, how much agreement should they have in their discernment? Is there a percentage to it, or just a feeling? Should there be no disagreement at all? What constitutes group unity?

10

Grace and Works
Galatians 3:6-7 and James 1:27; 2:21

Personal Preparation

1. Reflect on the previous nine sessions. Which of the sessions have been most striking, inspiring, or useful? Which have been the least? Why?
2. On one day, read Paul's letter to the Galatians. Mark the passages that center around faith and works. On a piece of paper or in a journal, write out the three or four verses that seem most important to you. Pray those verses, turning them into your own words, directed toward God.
3. On another day, read the letter of James. Once again, mark the passages that center around works and faith. On the same piece of paper or in your journal, write out the three or four verses that seem most important to you. Pray those verses, turning them into your own words directed toward God.

Suggestions for Sharing and Prayer

1. Greet one another upon arrival and share some of the activities and adventures of the past week. Take time to offer sentence prayers of praise and petition for one another, perhaps by moving one at a time into the center of the circle to be the focus of prayer.
2. Reflect as a group on this current study. Share some of your personal reflections on the various sessions. Which have had the greatest impact? What surprised you most?

What intrigued you most? What disturbed you most? What new insights have you gained? What lessons have you learned?

3. Make a list of the churches of various ethnicities that you have attended. What are some of the unique characteristics of worship in these congregations? What characteristics of worship, if any, seem to be universal? What languages were used? What customs or traditions were followed? What kinds of music or preaching styles set each church apart? What were your reactions as you worshiped in these various settings, and later upon reflection? What, if anything, might you suggest incorporating into your own congregational worship life?

4. This session marks the conclusion of this study. Set aside a time of silent reflection and intercessory prayer for one another. Talk about whether or not to continue meeting as a group after this session.

5. Draw this part of your gathering to a close by singing the hymn "In Christ there is no east or west."

Understanding

In some ways, writing this chapter felt a lot like a trip to the dentist. No matter how much I dreaded it, it still had to be done—and it felt so good when it was over! The controversy between faith and works was not settled by the Apostle Paul two thousand years ago—it is an essential tension and a constant contradiction that is still not settled within our heart of hearts.

If our salvation is by faith alone, can't we all just profess our faith in Jesus as our Lord and Savior and be done with it? If so, we could stay home on Sunday mornings, put our feet up and read the paper, and maybe eat leftovers and get some real rest on the sabbath.

If our salvation is by works alone, then does it really matter what we profess as long as we're doing the work of Jesus Christ? Do we even have to know about Jesus to do his work?

When Paul wrote his letter to Galatian Christians, faith in Jesus was still centered in Jerusalem. And many assumed a new Christian had to adopt Jewish cultural practices.

But in the Roman Empire, there were many different cultural practices. People didn't think the same way. To some, circumcision was not the mark of a covenant, but a disfigurement of a body that was beautiful. While worship of One God was attractive, the complex food laws made no sense when consumption of meat was a social practice that involved, at least technically, the worship of a pagan god.

Paul was advocating for the acceptance of new converts who would follow Jesus but not shed their own cultural and ethnic backgrounds. In today's terms, it was as if everyone had to become Irish or Italian or Ukrainian in order to become a follower of Jesus. Yet anyone who has lived in a multicultural setting knows that worship takes delightfully different forms in the African churches, in the many Hispanic traditions, among Asians of various sorts, as well as in all the different European varieties.

At the Jerusalem Council described in Acts 15, James the brother of Jesus and the other Jerusalem leaders met with Paul, Barnabas, and others to discuss the matter. The result, described both in Acts and in Galatians, seems to indicate that Paul "won." Salvation was by faith in Jesus, not in the acts of the believer.

Central to Paul's arguments was his interpretation of the Hebrew scriptures. According to Paul, Abraham acted by faith. There was no Hebrew law for him to obey. Paul quoted Genesis 15:6 to show that Abraham "believed God, and it was reckoned to him as righteousness" (Gal. 3:6).

If Paul won, James doesn't seem to know it. In his letter, James also refers to Abraham when he writes, "Was not our ancestor Abraham justified by works when he offered his son Isaac on the altar? You see that faith was active along with his works, and faith was brought to completion by the works. Thus the scripture was fulfilled that says, 'Abraham believed God, and it was reckoned to him as righteousness,' and he was called the friend of God. You see that a person is justified by works and not by faith alone" (James 2:21-24).

James also said, "If a brother or sister is naked and lacks daily food, and one of you says to them, 'Go in peace; keep warm and eat your fill,' and yet you do not supply their bodily needs, what is the good of that? So faith by itself, if it has no works, is dead" (James 2:15-17). And he wrote: "Religion that is pure and undefiled before God, the Father, is this: to care for orphans and widows in their distress, and to keep oneself unstained by the world" (James 1:27).

In examining this contradiction, I would first remind us that neither Paul nor James were twenty-first century North Americans. They were both Jewish citizens of an empire that spanned the western world and struggled with cultural assumptions that divided genders, races, social, and economic classes as a matter of course. Both were martyred for their faith.

As Jews, they believed there were Two Ways, a *yetzer ha'tov*, a good way, and a *yetzer ha'ra*, a bad way. They believed we are able to make choices between those two ways. But in one of those "same planet, different worlds" kind of things, they took those same building blocks and came to look at the world in different yet complementary ways.

Paul is constantly promoting good works. At the Jerusalem Conference, he agrees to take up a collection for the poor in Jerusalem. He speaks of that collection's importance in 2 Corinthians 8 and 9. On another trip to Jerusalem, one of his good deeds was to pay the fees to release four Christians from a Nazarite vow (Acts 21:24).

Faith in Jesus seems essential, but Jesus himself doesn't seem to care much about it. I do not recall a single verse in which he says of himself to proclaim his name and be saved. The Sermon on the Mount seems very works oriented. In Matthew 25:31-46, Jesus describes an end-time judgment scenario based totally on good works.

It seems to me that though most Christians give lip service to Paul's formulation about grace over law, they also believe in their hearts, as it is stated in Matthew 25 and James 1:27, that our works save us.

Does either extreme—faith or works—have much to do with faith in Jesus Christ? I have met Christians who insist that since they have "come forward" and expressed their faith in Jesus, they can no longer sin. They claim whatever they do is not a sin, whether it's ignoring a parent's medical condition, looking down with contempt on people of other races, or simply living in callous disregard of the sufferings of others around the world—they cannot be touched by reason or argument. They are never wrong.

On the other hand, I have met those who are so dedicated to the work of Jesus they'd be hard pressed to quote a single verse from a Gospel outside the Sermon on the Mount. Jesus becomes a convenient hat rack on which to hang their arguments.

If there is any conundrum associated with scripture, any apparent contradiction for which we should give thanks, it may be that the tension between faith and works is essential to building the real body of Christ. Every denomination, every small Bible study group, each race and ethnic enclave, all the Christians spread across every continent, should be pulling each other back and forth, challenging, teaching, and, most of all, loving each other.

Life is messy. It's never fully resolved. Things don't always have to work out. When it comes to the great questions, do we have to have an answer today, or can it wait until next Tuesday? Most of all, can we give ourselves time to work on these problems together?

Remember the thief on the cross? Was he saved by faith or works? Faith in what? There was no risen Lord—or even a fully crucified Jesus. Then was he saved by works? But he didn't do anything. He didn't rescue Jesus or alleviate his physical sufferings. The thief spoke.

I'm not going to try to settle whether the thief was saved by works or faith. I just know he's home free. And when it comes to the millions who serve Jesus by declarations of faith or words or actions or simply good intentions, I'm not going to try to settle exactly how the mechanism works that saves them.

I'm just going to praise God.

Discussion and Action

1. Look at the verses you wrote down as part of your Personal Preparation, and share aloud those which seem most important to your life. After reading the verses, tell why they are important to you.

2. If you were pushed to choose between faith and works, where would you find yourselves, as individuals and as a group?

3. What is your comfort level when it comes to visiting churches and faith groups that have a different orientation or practice than your own? Have you ever worshiped or worked with such groups? Tell stories about your experiences, and talk together about what you have learned in such settings.

4. In what ways does this group demonstrate faith in action? In what ways does this group demonstrate action in faith?

5. Having shared this Bible study, what can you say about the importance of walking through the scriptures together as a group versus individual study? What are the merits of each? What are the challenges? What can you learn in group discernment that you can't learn alone?

6. Consider ways that you might worship and work with Christians whose style and background are different from your own. Might a Sunday morning exchange program, where you go to visit other churches one Sunday and they reciprocate by attending your worship the next week, work for you? Or might it be possible to hold joint Bible studies or other special services with people from other backgrounds? What might you learn from one another?

7. Look ahead to your next study together. What will you be sharing? What hopes do you have for that study? What ways will this study influence the way you look at future group sessions? If any among you are aware they won't be participating in the next study, find a way to bless them and wish them well.

Other Covenant Bible Studies

Each book is $6.95 plus shipping and handling. For a full description of each title, ask for a free catalog of these and other Brethren Press titles. Major credit cards accepted. Prices subject to change. Regular Customer Service hours are Monday through Friday, 8 a.m. to 5 p.m. CT.

Brethren Press • 1451 Dundee Avenue • Elgin, Illinois 60120
Phone: 800-441-3712 Fax: 800-667-8188
e-mail: brethrenpress_gb@brethren.org
www.brethrenpress.com